LEGACY LIBRARY

MARIETTA COLLEGE
Marietta, Ohio

Gift of
the estate of
Rudolph P. Zalesak

ISABEL
BISHOP

SELF-PORTRAIT, 1984, Ink wash, 12 x 15½ inches, Collection of Mrs. Alan D. Gruskin

ISABEL BISHOP Helen Yglesias Foreword by John Russell

RIZZOLI
NEW YORK

This book is dedicated to Isabel Bishop,
who died during its preparation in February 1988.

A CHAMELEON BOOK

First published in the United States of America in 1988 by
RIZZOLI INTERNATIONAL PUBLICATIONS, INC.
597 Fifth Avenue
New York, NY 10017

Produced by Chameleon Books, Inc.
31 Smith Road, Chesterfield, Massachusetts 01012

Production director/designer: Arnold Skolnick
Editorial director: Marion Wheeler
Associate editors: Stephen Frankel, Vicki Brooks
Editorial assistant: Ellen Dibble
Design assistants: Nancy Crompton, Kathleen Unruh
Composition: David Seham Associates, Metuchen, New Jersey
Production services: Four Colour Imports, Ltd., Louisville, Kentucky
Printed and bound by Everbest Printing Company, Ltd., Hong Kong

The "Anthology of Drawings" section of this book was produced in
connection with an exhibition of drawings, etchings, and paintings
by Isabel Bishop, organized by the Edith C. Blum Art Institute of
Bard College, Annandale-on-Hudson, New York, and toured by the
Mid-America Arts Alliance, Kansas City, Missouri. Partners of the
M-AAA include the state arts agencies of Arkansas, Kansas,
Missouri, Nebraska, Oklahoma, and Texas, the National
Endowment for the Arts, and private sector contributors.

Library of Congress Cataloging-in-Publication Data:
Yglesias, Helen.
   Isabel Bishop.
   Bibliography: pp. 23, 148, 178.
   Includes index.
   1. Bishop, Isabel, 1902–1988—Criticism and
interpretation. I. Title.
ND 237.B594Y7 1988   759.13   88–42700
ISBN 0-8478-0976-5

CONTENTS

ACKNOWLEDGMENTS I was introduced to the work of Isabel Bishop by Lisa Baskin, to whom I am immeasurably indebted for my involvement with the subject and the woman. Isabel Bishop was herself most gracious of her time, her thoughts, her memories, and her philosophical approach to art, particularly throughout her last debilitating illness. In spite of physical difficulties due to the stroke she had suffered, she continued to meet with me and communicate at the clearest mental level. It was a privilege and a pleasure to spend time with her. Wherever I have not indicated other sources, all of the direct statements made by Isabel Bishop originated during the seven interviews I conducted with her in 1982, 1983, and 1987.

I am indebted also to Leonard Baskin for his enlightening views on art in general and on Isabel Bishop in particular. Marion Wheeler and Arnold Skolnick made a labor of love lighter and more rewarding, as did Bridget Moore, Mary Gruskin, and John and Joanne Whitney Payson of the Midtown Galleries. It is hard to express sufficient gratitude for Eleanor Munro's great generosity in sharing her findings and thoughts on Isabel Bishop, beyond what appeared in her innovative work, *Originals: American Women Artists*. Avis Berman and Cynthia Nadelman of the oral history division of the Archives of American Art were immensely helpful, as were courteous staff members in the print division and the reading room of The Pierpont Morgan Library. I am grateful to Jack Levine for a spirited conversation that provided me with invaluable information, and to Rosa Shimin, to Ruth and Robert Hatch, and finally, and especially, to Dr. Robert Ascheim for providing important pieces of the mosaic. It goes without saying that only I am responsible for any errors or clumsy stupidities in the text.

H.Y.

Chameleon Books is very grateful for the invaluable assistance provided by the directors and staff of Midtown Galleries. But for the cheerful and tireless creative collaboration of Mary Gruskin, Bridget Moore, Edward DeLuca, and Priscilla Greene, this book would not exist. We wish to acknowledge the fine work done by photographers Toby Old, Ed Watkins, Otto E. Nelson, Stephen Petegorsky, and Robert F. Haiko. And we thank our authors for writing so well about an artist we came to love as we worked on this book.

Not long after I came to live in New York, I saw a painting by Isabel Bishop of young women walking around. Almost without exception, they had books under their arms. They had a strong, easy, unregimented way of walking. It was *walking*, not marching, and they walked with head straight and eyes open.

They were mightily impressive. With that walk, and those books, they would make the world—and, not least, the nursery—a better place. The truth would set them free, and their liking for life-long perambulation would keep them well. There were young men in those images, too. How lucky they were to walk in the same country, the same city, and the same street as those direct, upright, well-oriented young women!

Later, I used sometimes to see Isabel Bishop herself in the subway. Tall, slender, and straight, she was a calming presence. (I did not yet know that she had prized the Art Students League in her early twenties because, as she once put it, "There were even fights at lunch.")

Riding those drab trains, she was impartially curious as to the looks, nature, and possible history of every one of our momentary companions. As recently as 1966, she had portrayed the subway station underneath Grand Central Station as a place in which people stood tall and walked free and had room to swing their arms, rather than as a place to get out of as fast as possible. And here she was still watching out for the young people who would one day deserve the keys of the city.

When the conductor called "Fourteenth Street, Union Square!" she got out, and I thought better of the day, and of the city, because I had seen her. To begin with, there were so many things that she was not. She was not aggressive, not sentimental, and not deceived. She knew the score, where this particular big city was concerned, but she did not despair or give up. Worrisome as many things were, she was still confident that one day, somehow, people, now very young, would change the lot of women in big cities for the better.

Also, she had a sense of continuity. Already in 1932, when she painted her *Dante and Virgil in Union Square*—a remarkable achievement, by the way, for someone just thirty years old—she saw in Union Square a timeless, universal quality. It was a place in which not only Dante and Virgil but Diogenes might one day pass by. It was an American agora, a place in which amateur logicians could argue the day away and know that they were part of a radical tradition that had drifted across the Atlantic from Athens and Rome. As for the bums—well, weren't there bums in Athens, too?

The difference was that in Union Square there were thinking women, as well as thinking men. Isabel Bishop was sensitive, all her life long, to those thinking women, many of whom were as yet unmarked by life. She was alert to the potential both for happiness and for an irrevocable, untold misery that exists at every stage of metropolitan life. In her work, she never lectured and rarely told an identifiable story. But, as she moved in and out of the unidentified lives that she set down on paper or canvas, her concerned good will was everywhere evident.

Her work related, as has often been said, to a specific and distinctly American tradition. Its idiom had been pioneered at the turn of this century by Robert Henri, Everett Shinn, George Luks, John Sloan, and others. It was carried forward by Kenneth Hayes Miller and Guy Pène du Bois (both of them former students of Robert Henri) and by Reginald Marsh. It was reportorial in style, anecdotal in tone, and shorn of all extraneous or merely complimentary material.

The truth mattered to all those artists, and their ideal was to tell it under the mask of entertainment. The work was intended to seize a moment, tell a tale, and give a renewed dignity to people for whom high art had not always had a place.

Isabel Bishop's work was not anecdotal in that sense. Where her men colleagues pinned people down and wrapped them up, she gave them a clear steady glance and went on her way. She was of her own day, but for all the rapid, spontaneous, instinctive quality of her observation she knew how to reach back into European Old Master painting and drawing and printmaking for support and encouragement. John I. H. Baur, former director of the Whitney Museum of American Art, once said of her that "in some mysterious manner which I do not really understand, her paintings carry forward the great tradition of north European seventeenth-century figure painting."

Others saw an American derivation. Reginald Marsh was a close friend of Isabel Bishop's, and he once said that her art "cuts to the truth. It is at once original and traditional, as is that of Thomas Eakins." Either way, it was the truth that counted for her. And that truth was in everyday things and in what many would consider to be everyday people, as much as in the huge commotions of Old Master painting.

Talking to Cindy Nemser in 1976, Isabel Bishop traced her absorption in everyday sights to the years of her childhood, when her father moved his family from Princeton to Detroit. In Princeton, he had had a small school of his own. When they moved to Detroit, it turned out that although the

ISABEL BISHOP— HER LIFE AND WORK

school was bigger and grander, the salary did not allow the family to live anywhere but in what she called "a very lower, lower-class neighborhood."

We were very isolated in Detroit and had almost no social life. I wasn't supposed to play with the children on my block, but I wanted to. I thought, they have a warmer life than we do— they all see each other, and we are isolated.

After an experience of that sort, New York life— even in its more somber aspects—had an affirmative quality. So did the particular perseverance of those New Yorkers who stayed in the city, craved no other place in the world, and radiated an unchanging and fanatically held belief in the pursuit of painting as something absolutely important, irrespective of the degree of talent or of any external circumstances whatever.

Isabel Bishop had that kind of commitment. As she once said to Eleanor Munro, "One simply found oneself in a state of commitment. And after that, there wasn't any choice—except jumping off a roof." There is no way to counterfeit that commitment, and Isabel Bishop never needed to. In her own sole self, she spoke for an uncorrupted art world in which what mattered was neither the acclaim nor the prices at auction, but the work. In that, she set a glorious example.

John Russell

ISABEL BISHOP, 1937

Isabel Bishop died in February 1988. Born in 1902, she bowed out of our overblown century in her characteristically quiet ladylike style. Funeral services were held at Christ Church in Riverdale (the church that she more or less regularly attended), where Holy Eucharist was celebrated followed by the taking of Communion, a ritual that she herself had often observed. Mourners included her only son and two granddaughters and a mixed congregation of Riverdale neighbors and Manhattan art world people. No representative of the art world spoke. She and her career were eulogized by the priest conducting the church ceremony. There were reminiscences, and readings from her favorite poet, Gerard Manley Hopkins. Mourners filed in and out of the church, conscious of the stained-glass window commemorating her husband, Dr. Harold Wolff, the eminent neurologist whom she had married in 1934 and who had died in 1962. A reception followed at the Riverdale family home. She had set up her last studio there after she gave up her lifelong Union Square working space with the onset of illness in 1984. Bishop's Riverdale home is rich in family mementos and enhanced by the accumulated treasures of her long and distinguished career in the arts—the mutual exchanges between artists who are good friends, of portraits and self-portraits, of sketches, prints, drawings, and paintings that so abundantly cover its walls.

There is a fascinating dichotomy at the heart of the story of this most remarkable painter, a story that tells itself best, as in some of her most notable works, in couplings, in contrasts, in pairs, and in opposites. "Only a proposition has meaning if its opposite has meaning," was one of the quotes she kept taped to her easel to test the validity of a painting, a concept that is applicable to her life as well. For this artist, who has given us, among other powerful images, our most aesthetically satisfying and lasting projections of a particular segment of American life—Union Square, the unemployed, women on their work breaks, confiding over a book, sharing a drink and an ice-cream cone, paring their nails or undressing on a bed, riding the subway to and from the shops, offices and restaurants where they worked, the subway itself as place and as state of soul, thus creating an opus of a quintessential city humanity, besieged, resigned, yet vibrantly beautiful—this artist lived and died supported by solid, upper middle-class amenities among devoted family members and many friends, with the recognition, the awards and the critical acclaim of the establishment.

There is no question here of "discovery" or "rediscovery." Isabel Bishop has been apparent inside and outside the art establishment from her earliest days in the 1930 s. But even within this generally respectful recognition there seems to have been a concerted diminution of her gifts and of her importance. "Read in, from small to large," was another quote taped to her easel. It is as if this motto were turned around by some viewers determined to read into her work, from small to smallest.

Bishop rooted her philosophy of art in one of two concepts of the world—the first an organization of disparate and disconnected parts and the other a mobile, essentially comprehensible, causal, and continuous pattern. It is the second—the world of continuity—that has governed her point of view. "Art is above all the artist's view of the world, the artist's view of life. Form forms itself, on that basic concept," she told me. Translated into artistic terms, she felt that the connected view was personified in the art of the Baroque and that she had the most to learn, technically, from its practitioners.

As in many of Bishop's theoretical stances, one may agree or disagree, but her ideas are an invaluable key to the persuasive work in which the smallest of her subjects are powered with a vitalizing and towering humanity. They are also a key to understanding how the life she lived was maintained in such striking opposition to the subject matter she chose.

Two images come to mind.

It is 1918. Sixteen-year-old Isabel Bishop arrives in New York, alone, to live in a "chaperoning establishment" for young women on the Upper East Side and to study illustration at the New York School of Applied Design. It is the heyday of illustration, and her hope is to make her living through this skill. She had demonstrated some talent for drawing back home in Detroit—"the only talent I ever had," she insisted years later with characteristic modesty. A relative is paying her way, which is an encouragement but also a pressure. Self-doubt weighs on her but she also harbors a stubborn will to succeed. She is frightened, lonely, fascinated, hopeful, excited. She explores every street, immersing herself in the magic of New York City, which she instantly loves, but there are other moments, when the overpowering density of the city bears down upon her with isolating oppression. She is surrounded in her eminently respectable boarding house for young women by well-bred provincial art and music students like herself. They are certainly as unsure and ignorant as she is. She determines to stick it out among these neophytes. She will study, study, study, and learn, learn, learn.

The year of the second image is 1984. A well-groomed, impeccably neat woman in her eighties steps out of a beautifully old-fashioned home in Riverdale onto a sloping red brick path, leading to a tree-lined street that winds its way past other charming homes until it reaches Broadway and the 242nd Street station of the IRT subway.

Riverdale is an enclave of good living that is embedded at the tip of the Bronx, a borough of New York City large and diverse enough to hold within its borders this surprising oasis in what is elsewhere a hive of working-class activity and a rubble of urban decay. Riverdale divides into new and old Riverdale, the new embracing high-rise condominiums and shopping malls, the old clinging to individual homes and homeowners, with Riverdale society splitting down the middle. New York City's most elite prep schools are housed in Riverdale; and there is a yacht club on the Hudson, without any yachts, but bestowing much prestige on its privileged members.

The incongruous come together at the foot of the elevated train, suburban Riverdale vanishing at the staircase leading to the platform. Here the underground rides above ground. The subway cars that rumble to a stop after a short wait are wildly covered with grafitti, outside and in, but this woman of measured step and stooped back boards the train with absolute naturalness. She is on her way to a studio in Union Square, an area which has consistently been the habitat of her art since 1922, throughout all the years of social agitation and violent changes that have visited this volatile area.

A span of sixty-six years separates the two images. The geographical and social lines are disparate—but this coming and going with rigid regularity between opposite worlds, this sixty-six years of treading a narrowly demarcated path, accommodated a life's work of astonishingly rich breadth, depth, and lasting beauty.

Like all artists, Isabel Bishop invented herself. In the persona she created there were no boldly theatrical elements, none of the flamboyance of a Louise Nevelson, the melodramatic biography of an Alice Neel, the geo-sexual imagery of Georgia O'Keeffe, nor was there the pervasive presence of a powerful artist husband or father, as is so often the case with women artists. All the elements of her biography were proper, correct. She projected a facade of the dignified "lady," always polite, undemanding, modest, and thoughtful of others, who lived a well-ordered existence in the best of all possible worlds. In our meetings to talk together in 1982, 1983, and in 1987, only weeks before she died, I was greeted by the same reserved, self-contained, polite woman.

Always meticulously groomed, even during the

last days of her life, her hair smoothly done, her skin surprisingly luminous and unlined, Isabel Bishop was the epitome of the perfect lady, the perfect hostess. Although her back was so stooped—it was by then almost a hump—and her long, articulated fingers barely functioned, she served me Pepperidge Farm cookies on lovely English china and sherry in a beautifully worked glass. In the studio she had worn a smock which was a doctor's jacket; now at home seated in an armchair in her study where she had been placed by her nurse, she was as carefully dressed and groomed as ever. Too shaky after a stroke to lift a cup to her lips, she nevertheless made sure that coffee or tea and cookies were served to visitors on an impeccably appointed tray.

It would be perverse and ungenerous to describe this manner as an affectation, although such formality may arouse a certain discomfort in the visitor, and some wonder. Where is the artist in this controlled personality and atmosphere?

When I first visited Isabel Bishop in her Union Square studio, she was already in her eighties. Although she was not familiar with my work and had no reason to trust me, she was pleased that I was then writing a brief appreciation for a special woman-in-the-arts issue of *The Massachusetts Review*. There were subsequent visits to Union Square and to the Riverdale home where she later moved her studio. Each encounter found her unfailingly cordial, kind, intelligent, and responsive, but there was always a distance set between us— a space, exactly defined and exactly maintained— in which her inviolability was reserved. Our talks remained careful, measured. Yet I discerned that under the mannerisms, there lurked subversion and a passionate intensity. In search of this subversive element, I pursued Isabel Bishop beyond her canvases.

Isabel Bishop was born into a family that already included two sets of twins. The late child of her parents, she was even further isolated from participation in the exclusive relationships among her brothers and sisters by a thirteen-year gap in age between her and the younger twins. When she spoke of her childhood, without openly straying from her usual cheerful demeanor, the account was stained by a dark Victorian tinge of unmentionable and perhaps not clearly understood unhappiness. In such a family conformation, it was inevitable that she would feel herself "different."

The youngest member in a family often labors under a feeling of being handicapped by a late entrance into an already hardened family history. There had been five children ahead of Isabel Bishop (one baby died); her mother and father had begun a marriage long before she was born in which they had hoped to combine youth, energy, intellectual accomplishment, and wage earning in a good and productive life. Together they had founded a prep school in Princeton. Soon after, the first set of twins were born, and it became too much for her mother: caring for the babies, running a household, helping with the administration of the school, and teaching. The young couple gave up their dream of running a school and moved to Cincinnati. At first her father could get work only as a teacher in the public education system, but in time he became the principal of the Walnut Hills School.

The child Isabel was aware of ups and downs in the family fortunes, of perhaps too much moving about, of a scent of failure permeating her well-educated father's efforts. They were middle-class but precariously so; there was not enough money to fulfill middle-class demands easily. A rich relative, her father's cousin James Bishop Ford, came to their aid at crucial moments, the relative who would stake Isabel Bishop to her career as an artist. She reported a vivid memory of the family moving to Detroit when her father took yet another job in another school. The family settled in a marginal area bordering on a working-class district, and, although young Isabel was forbidden to play with the children of the workers, she watched them from the window of her house, envying them the color and warmth of their community.

Her mother was a Suffragist and feminist who hated housework and did not really enjoy children. Above all, she urged her daughters to become independent, but what the daughter remembered was her mother's indifference.

I wanted to be special. I always wanted more than I got. I overheard her say one day she felt more like a grandmother to me. I hated that. I wanted a mother.

Bishop recognized later that this mother who distanced herself from her last child was really a person of passionate intelligence whose conventional upbringing had held her back. But at the time her sympathies were torn between father and mother in the face of their differences.

Father was an Episcopalian believer, a regular Sunday church goer. Mother thought that Christianity was a mistake, a minor sect. She was totally against the church. She always said if there'd been no Middle Ages, we would still be living as the Greeks did. I don't remember the details (I was about eight or ten years old), but Mother had to testify in court about something or other and she refused to take the oath on the Bible. "I don't believe in God," she said. It caused a scandal. I felt so sorry for my father. I thought it was terrible of her.

Her mother wanted to be a writer, but she had no luck in publishing what she produced. She taught herself Italian in order to do a new English translation of Dante's *Inferno*.

All the years of my growing up, she was totally absorbed in translating Dante. I recognize now that she was living with the disappointment of wanting to be a writer and of never getting published. But I was so mixed up then. My siblings were so much older than I, they were more like parents. They would go off to college and when they came home they'd pick up their interest in me, like a parent—decide what kind of person I should be. One of my sisters had me in Eton collars and tunics; then she went off and another came home and disapproved of those dull clothes and put me in some fancy little things. Everyone was trying to do something to me, except my mother. She was indifferent. My father adopted me as his special interest. He saw the family as divided into two groups, "we" and "they." Mother and my sisters and brothers were on one side, and my father and I were on the other. I didn't like that. I hated it.

One of her sisters, older by fifteen years, was a gifted artist. "She drew well, better than I did, but she didn't pursue it."

Bishop's father was ousted from his position in Detroit for incompetence, it was claimed, although she remembered the event as a political scandal in which he was innocently caught up.

It broke his heart. I feared for him. Then his wonderful rich cousin saved us again, used his influence to set father up as dean of faculty at a military academy he had endowed, and he even supplied a house on campus. But it was humiliating for father. He told himself that he had come to the academy to teach Greek and Latin, but he knew that he had been forced on the faculty and that no one was interested in his scholarship.

A brother was killed in action while serving in the Air Force in World War I. His twin went to China as an Episcopal missionary nurse, eventually coming home ill with a tropical disease. One of the other set of twins became a high-school teacher in Detroit. "The other never did much of anything," Bishop told me. Many years later after the death of her father, her mother and a sister and her sister's husband bought the house directly next door to her own house in Riverdale. The Bishops would become something of a family again.

Isabel Bishop was twelve when she was enrolled in a Saturday morning art class in Detroit.

It was a shock to walk into class and find a great fat nude woman posing. The theory was that it was best to learn to draw from life. When

I got to New York and my classes at the School of Applied Design for Women, I considered myself an experienced student, so they put me directly into the life class. I skipped learning how to lay in a wash, perspective, and all those other things. Sometimes I wish I'd studied them.

She was still living at the Misses Wilde's establishment on the Upper East Side.

Our parents didn't know it but the chaperonage was nonexistent. We kept the Misses Wilde utterly bewildered. "But, dear, we would like to meet the young man," they would say. "Oh Miss Jenny, that's not at all necessary," was the standard answer. I stayed there two years, beyond the end of the war. I remember us art students in our smocks, walking in the Armistice Day parade. Then I learned about modern art and put commercial art behind me. I enrolled at the Art Students League and moved to the Village with two other girls.

During the First World War, the memory of the Armory Show of 1913 that had blasted American art into the era of modernism had dimmed, but with the end of the war the excitement of this revolutionary art happening was rekindled, particularly among the younger artists such as Isabel Bishop, who had missed the event. At the Société Anonyme, which was located on East Forty-seventh Street in Manhattan, Katherine Dreier championed Surrealism and the Dada movement. A formidable personality, Katherine Dreier was a Suffragist and bountiful supporter of advanced European art and artists, particularly Marcel Duchamp, whose *Nude Descending a Staircase* was the most celebrated single canvas in the Armory Show. Isabel Bishop found this ambience "an inspiration" and her later immersion in the chaotic intellectual turmoil of the Art Students League wonderfully liberating.

The loose organization at the League allowed the young artist the freedom to pick and choose among the teachers. Isabel Bishop started with Max Weber's class in late Cubism, but Weber's arrogance intimidated her. He disliked her work, criticizing it savagely before the other students. She found that hard to bear and not useful. She moved on to study with Kenneth Hayes Miller. Quite apart from his output, Kenneth Hayes Miller commanded a special place in American art. He was one of the most influential teachers of a generation of painters, which included, before him, realist Robert Henri of the Ash Can school, after him, abstract expressionist Hans Hofmann.

When Isabel Bishop began to study under Miller, she was just eighteen and still clinging to the unexamined expectation that it was natural to be "taught," to be "influenced," to be "helped." She readily absorbed Miller's philosophy, which

was based on his idea of artistic commitment. Quite apart from talent, Miller taught his students, what was required to be a serious artist was total dedication, an attribute he exemplified in his own person. Dedication to work, work, work was probably his most lasting gift to Bishop. Commitment was so integral a part of Miller's teaching that by the time Bishop became aware of the vital growth of dedication within her, she could not logically account for the implantation of the seed. Miller had shown at the Armory, his radicalism evidenced by the positing of "ordinary" American subjects rendered in the classic forms and surfaces of the great masters. The subject might be a shop girl but the figure's stance would suggest monumentalism and the palette would glow with Rubenesque color. According to Bishop,

he was exploring in his own way, an entirely different way. He was intellectually stimulating, not stultifying, a fascinating person who presented all sorts of new possibilities, new points of view. It was possible to stay with him and still be open to other influences.

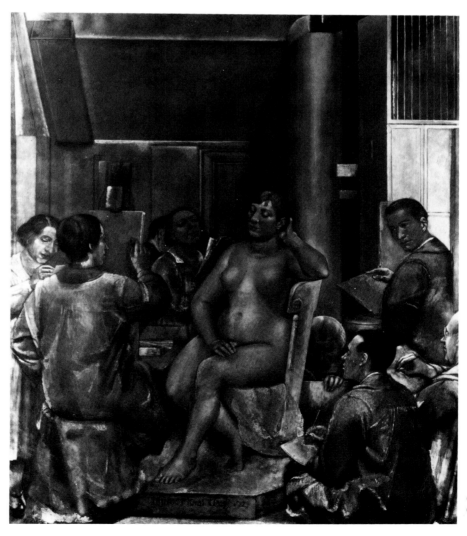

KENNETH HAYES MILLER
MURAL CLASS, ART
STUDENTS LEAGUE, 1927
Oil on canvas, 82½ x 72
Collection of The Art Students
League of New York

Reginald Marsh, who became a close friend, also greatly admired Kenneth Hayes Miller. Marsh was four years older than Bishop and a recent graduate of Yale, where he had been big-man-on-campus as well as an editor at the *Yale Record*. After his arrival in New York, he quickly got a job reviewing burlesque shows for the *Daily News*. He kept in close touch with Miller and was in and out of the League, where Bishop and Marsh met. Marsh took young Isabel to the sites he celebrated and satirized in his own works—Coney Island, the dressing rooms of self-service discount stores on Fourteenth Street, and backstage at Minsky's, the major burlesque house of the day. Bishop enjoyed the jaunts but did not follow his lead in using such subject matter.

Bishop's eagerness to soak up the atmosphere of intellectualism that she felt all about her in the great city had sparked an independent seriousness in her naturally inquisitive, intelligent mind. If she bent to Miller's strong exclusive ideas of form and content—the form classic, the content commonplace, American, contemporary—she remained open to other mentors. Guy Pène du Bois, an elegant and satiric painter of New York City café life, another teacher at the League, also became Bishop's close friend. Du Bois had lived in Paris and exuded an airier, more sophisticated artistic approach, one antipathetic to Miller's views. "I was influenced spiritually by Dub, more by his point of view than by his painting, which is very beautiful and underrated now," she told me.

Between these conflicting views, Isabel Bishop tentatively sought her own way. In the historic struggle for woman's liberation, progress has been made in a spiral of ups and downs. The twenties were one of the rising points. It was a period when women were very active in the arts; there was for her no sense of being seen as inferior because she was a young woman. Yet a crippling unspoken plea for help operated unconsciously within her, as it does with many women, welling up as the result of societal pressure that designates the female organically incapable of independence. All human beings crave communion, males as well as females; it is a natural and intense human need. But women are tempted to solve problems through an exploitative misuse of emotions which are muddied by discriminatory dicta of male-female roles, and men, out of their own distorted needs, are often happy to indulge such unspoken pleas. Bishop continued to lean on the generous male relative who supplied her economic wants for many years, and it is interesting that she saw her gender not as a drawback but working to her advantage here:

I was lucky. I think if I had been a man the relative who sponsored my whole studenthood might not have done so. Men are supposed to make their own way. Young women were supposed to marry. But a young woman putting so much time and effort—being so serious— that was different—that interested him. I don't think he would have subsidized me if I had been a boy.

Was it not equally natural to look to powerful artistic figures to help shape her work? Although there were friendships with many of the women artists of our century—Peggy Bacon, Minna Citron, Katherine Schmidt, Ruth Gikow, Alice Neel, Louise Nevelson, to name only a few—it was her fellow male students who would be the major influences.

It was Edward Laning, also a member of Miller's class in mural painting, who lettered the quote from Henry James's short story of an artist, "The Middle Years," that hung in her studio throughout her long sojourn on Union Square. It served as the credo to set her in motion day after self-doubting day:

We work in the dark. We do what we can— we give what we have. Our doubt is our passion, and our passion our task. The rest is the madness of art.

And it was Guy Pène du Bois who walked into her studio and, viewing the canvasses she was then working on in the Kenneth Hayes Miller tradition, demanded to know what the hell she thought she was doing, thus shocking her into the realization that she had "lost track entirely of the idea that to be an artist was to say something for oneself."

When she had left Detroit, she told me, at the age of sixteen, it was with the notion that *art* was what was hung in the local museum, that the task of an artist was to learn how to make that sort of painting, to learn from old masters what was beautiful to paint, and then to paint it. Once in New York, Bishop responded to the many artistic influences and currents surging around her, and art became a problem of discovery—"an intellectual pursuit of possible new dimensions and original thought." Art had become close, wrenching, private, an immensely difficult probing into the heart of a personal vision.

Isabel Bishop decided to work on her own. She left the League and rented her first studio on Union Square, where she set up housekeeping alongside her work space.

I didn't want to be part of anybody else's home then, but later I was in trouble, it was too isolating, too terrifying. It was a time of freedom for women to do what they wanted to do, but freedom can be intimidating. I was very young, in my early twenties, and my commitment to high art frightened me. It was an intellectual choice then, a deliberate choice. But that didn't keep it from being scary.

By the time Isabel Bishop settled into her studio on Union Square the area was no longer a fashionable section of a rapidly changing New York City. The mansions, elegant department stores, and restaurants were gone, as were the wealthy families such as the Henry James, Seniors, who had made their home at 58 West Fourteenth Street, shopped for groceries at the Jefferson Market, and sent their sons William and Henry to play in a Union Square enclosed like an English park by a wrought iron fence.

By the 1920s commercial buildings housing small industries and offices predominated. Hundreds of workers poured out into the streets surrounding the square during their breaks and lunch hours and on their way to and from their homes, traveling the intricate subway system whose hub was Union Square. S. Klein, an innovative department store that offered quality

merchandise at bargain prices, prefiguring the giant discount and self-service stores of today, dominated the eastern end of the square. Rival stores competed on Fourteenth Street: Hearns, Ohrbachs, Lerners. Although the luxury restaurant Luchow's clung to Fourteenth Street and Eva La Galliene's repertory theater remained active there for some years, Fourteenth Street, when Bishop first came to it, was not physically different from its current seedy, rundown incarnation, except for the presence today of drug dealers and street vendors.

By the early thirties, when Bishop first took the square itself as a subject, its historic role as a public meeting ground and center of political activity was still manifest. Soap-box speakers of all political, religious, and social persuasions pleaded their causes in the park, the square itself serving as a major demonstration site for unemployment protests or organized labor rallies that sought a living wage and a measure of security for workers. The massive May Day parades that annually displayed New York City's radical aspirations always ended at Union Square Plaza, in clear view of Isabel Bishop's studio windows. She did not march in these events, nor did she become a member of the graphics centers that prepared the wonderfully colorful banners and floats for the parade, but she was intimate with many of the artists who did.

Historically, a heady mix of democratic ferment amid an artistic ambience has imbued Union Square with its special qualities. In 1783 when the British evacuated New York City, George Washington was hailed by a huge crowd at the southeastern end of the square, where an equestrian statue of Washington by Henry Kirke Brown now more or less marks the spot. The square was the scene of many pro-Abolitionist demonstrations preceding and during the Civil War, and a statue of Lincoln, also by Brown, is at the upper end of the park. In the twenties, thousands gathered there in silent mourning for the executions of the anarchists Sacco and Vanzetti. By the 1950s, a peace demonstration was disrupted by police on horseback, and some protesters were beaten and arrested. A few years later mourners, protesting the execution of Ethel and Julius Rosenberg, were entirely forbidden the square and herded into the side streets.

The square's connection with the art world goes back to 1870 when the Metropolitan Museum of Art was first established and temporarily housed at Fifth Avenue and Fourteenth Street. In 1875, the Art Students League set itself up at Fifth Avenue and Sixteenth Street, moving to Fourteenth Street in 1882. Later, both the museum and the school moved uptown permanently. But what made Union Square a haven for artists in the twenties and thirties had as much to do with economics as anything else. The area offered an irresistible combination of space and affordable rents. So many artists moved into these spaces that by the 1920s a true artists' community existed in which it was possible to work, to play, to eat, to talk, to drink, and to socialize alongside one's artist friends.

Artists seldom concern themselves with "schools," and, when they do, it is usually in fun or to outrage established sensibilities. To speak therefore of the importance of Union Square in the work of Isabel Bishop—or of the Ash Can school or of the Fourteenth Street school—is to artificially settle her within limitations that cannot encompass her scope, her depth, or even her surface. Although the school of Robert Henri, Luks, and Shinn and the school of Miller and Marsh influenced her choice of subject, Bishop often attributed her use of shop girls and bums to the simple fact that "they were there."

Isabel Bishop did not feel herself part of a group. She came to the Art Students League four years after the class that had produced Alexander Brook and his wife Peggy Bacon, Kuniyoshi and his wife Katherine Schmidt. "I envied them. They were friends. They used to bowl in Teutonia Hall every Tuesday under Fourteenth Street. But I wasn't part of it."

She was working very hard, producing a great deal, not yet fully committed to the subject matter that became her unique terrain, although there were intimations. The earliest nudes are designs, somewhat cubist, showing little sign of the classic mastery of the later magnificently mature works. The large outdoor scenes of this period contained the chunky figures in the mode put forward by Miller and robustly executed by Reginald Marsh. It is these gesso panels that she literally destroyed with a hatchet in the seventies.

So much painstaking labor went into the work I did under Miller's teaching. And they were so awful, so terribly awful. He was teaching the concept of mural painting or Renaissance style. I made an overmantle showing people in a room standing this way and that, posed. There was an elaborate chandelier. It was just an exercise. It had no meaning.

Added to the pain of personal searching was the pain of reevaluating a revered mentor. Ambivalent judgments tore at Bishop. There was a literal life-and-death need to work free of a hindering influence, yet her admiration and gratitude were firm enough to surface again in an article on Miller written in 1952 for the *Magazine of Art:*

. . . . in America art is an underground move-

ment. . . . It explains the potency of the symbol those few artists and teachers become, whose almost saintlike unself-interestedness and singleness of purpose give them the position of Chiefs of the Underground. Miller was one of these.

The question of her commitment was by this time beside the point, certainly beyond discussion.

I realized that no matter how awful I felt about everything, the decision was made. I was ready to try anything to support my painting. I would teach, do commissioned portraits, anything. There were times when I came close to throwing myself out the window. But I went on. I felt I had no other choice.

I did things I had no true ability for, portraits from daguerrotypes for an old people's home near Peekskill. I used the best old master techniques, glazes and all, and made an honest effort to make them right, but bad works are bad, like those murals and overmantles. They looked absurd. Not psychologically true. But it was good discipline and I felt very good the one year I paid an income tax and felt I'd really earned money.

When she was twenty-four, a love affair came to an end. She tried to kill herself in three separate attempts. "I jumped into the Hudson River in the middle of the night," she told Sally Moore in an interview in 1975 for *People* magazine. "But my body just wouldn't die. It began to swim."

SHOWING MISUNDERSTANDING OF KENNETH HAYES MILLER'S TEACHING BY ONE OF HIS PUPILS, c. 1925
Medium and size unknown
Painting destroyed

LAFAYETTE, c. 1930
Pencil, 6½ x 6¾ inches
Collection of Malcolm Holzman

Union Square Studies, c. 1930
Pencil, 8½ x 6 inches
Courtesy of Midtown Galleries, New York

Love and art, and the anguish that attaches to each. Remarkably, the work of this period reveals nothing of this storm of emotion. No histrionics, no dramatics, no autobiography on canvas. There were a few admirable still lifes, a subject she did not explore further. And in the sketches, drawings, and etchings of the period 1927 to 1929, demonstrable, permanently recognizable Bishop gifts emerged: mobility in the figures conveyed by her idiosyncratic nervous line; the transparent seamless web of the surface of her paintings; her preoccupation with coats, the model putting on the coat, taking it off. Union Square made its entrance, the park wall, the statuary and the base of the flagpole, the idle men standing, sitting, and leaning in Union Square Park. These works reveal Bishop's fascination with the body deformed by ordinary clothing, what she describes as the "armor" of the male body: illfitting pants, clutzy shoes, jackets, coats, caps, brimmed hats, even strangling ties. The human longing for an ideal of community and comradeship, which flowers in her later studies of women in pairs, also made its first appearance, here shown operating primarily between males.

"Then for myself, I did heads, of myself, because I was there."

At the age of twenty-five, she produced the profoundly beautiful *Self-Portrait* of 1927 [p. 37] and the distinct way that Isabel Bishop *sees* was made manifest: the seeing beyond the image into what is psychologically true, revelatory in its humanity and clarity of emotion. The 1927 *Self-Portrait* was the first important instance of Bishop's series of self-portraits in the great tradition, culminating in her mid-eighties with her final, intensely honest probing of the self done a few years before she died [p. 41]. In these masterpieces, as in the female nudes, she is unique among American women painters, working within a vision closer to the Europeans Käthe Kollwitz and Paula Modersohn-Becker than to any American who comes to mind.

What is invaluable in her vision is that she is a woman painting self-portraits and female nudes. She would dislike any formulation that leaned on gender, even though she had said,

Critics could look at women's work from the point of view of finding content different from men's there, whether the women have consciously put it there or not . . . the work would have it if it's genuine.

The 1927 canvas is unlike a male self-portrait in that it tells us something different about the sitter, who is a female, particularly in the modeling that positions the hand at the cheek with the little finger tenderly stroking the lip. Yet like a Rembrandt or a Van Gogh self-portrait, the artist is seen without coquetry or dissimulation, seen as a quintessentially human subject. The little finger on the lip speaks of vulnerability; the intelligent eyes look out warily but eagerly; the small, exposed ear is listening. The image is reading us at the same time that we are reading it. We meet, spectator and model, head on, in a confrontation profoundly humanist and supremely feminist.

The 1934 *Nude* [p. 44] makes the same direct challenge to our sense of the female and presents as revolutionary a solution. The woman simply *is*; she exists as herself in her body. She is presented as a nude human being, unencumbered by the sexual and societal comment that surrounds and distorts her representations by male painters, whether through idealization or misogyny. In a Bishop painting, the nude is an essence of female we have not seen before because she has never been looked at and rendered in quite this way— for herself and for her unique humanity.

For Bishop this was a time of intense isolation, broken for a while by her involvement in the Whitney Studio Club where she had been introduced by Guy Pène du Bois. "It was a real center. I showed my still lifes there. I was thrilled. Lovely, it was lovely."

And then, in the early thirties, Alan Gruskin, fresh out of Harvard, full of enthusiasm for the new American artists but without any money to speak of, somehow pulled together a cooperative gallery. He housed it in gallery space at Fifth Avenue and Forty-ninth Street that had previously shown Old Masters and invited thirty or so young artists to participate in a continuous group show at a cost of five dollars a month for each artist. The Midtown Galleries began at the beginning of the Depression, when solidly established galleries were closing down. Isabel Bishop became one of Gruskin's artists and never moved to another gallery.

Mary Gruskin, in her eighties and still active as director emeritus in the gallery her husband founded, which was acquired in 1985 by John Whitney Payson and is now located on East Fifty-seventh Street, remembers Alan showing her a Bishop still life for her opinion, some time in the early thirties. She thought it must be the work of a highly accomplished, well-established painter and recalls Gruskin's gratification in correcting her assumption. "She's a young girl, Isabel Bishop, and she's going places."

The artist herself hardly shared his assurance. In our conversations, she could not recall a sense of being highly praised then, either by her teachers or by the critics. The catalogue of her first exhibition carried a foreword by Reginald Marsh, but his words of praise seem now to be marred by a tone of condescension, those of a lofty master bending to pat the neophyte on her well-behaved head:

Isabel Bishop is a very excellent example of what I feel is the right trend in American painting. She has studied with great diligence the classic tradition in Western painting and is employing it on the environment around her. She has successfully fused these two elements. To such commonplaces as modern men's clothing she has given the classic structure of beautiful engraving as no one else of today does. Every object is drawn with great care for its authentic shape and the part it is to play in the whole design. This intense positive study of each object for itself, in a world which is new to the painter's brush, is of immense value to American painting, which is all too shot with meaningless French mannerisms.

The values she and Marsh shared were more gracefully and generously expressed in Bishop's presentation speech on the occasion of Reginald Marsh being awarded the Gold Medal for Graphic Arts by the American Academy of Arts and Letters. This was in 1954, a few months before Marsh died.

You, whose work is so strongly contemporary, show that you connect yourself with the great past. . . . The persons you present in your pictures are little people, in unheroic situations. A shop girl, or perhaps she is a stenographer, strolls before highstooped rooming houses; casual groups are seen shopping, or in the street or park; a drunken man lounges; young people dive from a North River pier. They are nobodies—anybodies. . . . But they are modeled in the grand manner.

Here is ambiguity that counts for art: the un-pretty, insignificant, small, seemingly selected from our 160,000,000 people for their very lack of importance, given, without distortion or aggrandizement, "important" form and energy of presentation.

That speaks eloquently of her own work as well, and it is interesting that in another piece on Marsh, an introduction to his etchings, engravings, and lithographs, compiled by Norman Sasowsky in 1956, she discusses the value of "transparency," a consummation she achieves with stunning effect in her own work.

Bishop's association with fellow artists clearly nourished her. She traveled to Europe in 1931 with Kenneth Hayes Miller, Reginald Marsh, and Edward Laning, once again through the largesse of her generous relative. Under Miller's leadership, she studied the techniques of the great masters at the prestigious museums on the Continent and in England. "It was a working trip," she corrected my suggestion that such a jaunt must have been great fun. "I thought I was working very hard. I saw more of the museums than I did of the cities." On reflection she admitted, with a remarkably youthful smile, that the trip had been fun. It was during this tour that she first sketched outdoors, in Green Park in Antwerp, a development which she described as "the beginning of my art life." It was on her return to Union Square that she did her first drawings there.

She refers to the male Union Square habitués as "bums," a term now considered purely pejorative, but which was, during the 1930s, more a simple description of the rootless, working-class unemployed, as today's "yuppie" characterizes the young, upwardly mobile middle class. Unemployment cut such a wide swath of devastation through American society that to be a "bum" then was almost an occupation, allowing for the fellowship of cronies in a neighborhood park, card playing, story swapping, and group exploration of possible social panaceas for the communal pain they were experiencing. It was an acceptable private solution to "bum" across country, to ride the rails in boxcars or on the roofs of trains, seeing and getting the feel of America, picking up an occasional piece of work wherever one could and then moving on, much as the beats of the 1950s would hit the road, and the dropouts of the 1960s would search for answers to their social problems in drugs and in the rituals and magic of other cultures. In that sense, in picturing her "bums" in Union Square, Bishop had fallen upon a universal American subject, not because of a schematic attachment to "social significance," but through a more personal vision of the "importance of the particularity of what I was looking at," as she herself described it.

It would be almost perverse not to make a psychological connection between the child at the window longing to join the working-class children at play across the street from the respectable family home in Detroit and the artist Isabel Bishop at her wide studio window overlooking the square, enchanted by the sight below of the bums and working girls in the sustained action of their daily lives; or the psychological connection between the mysterious beauty of *Virgil and Dante in Union Square* and the web of complex emotions spun of her resentment over her mother's lifelong preoccupation with translating Dante.

Virgil and Dante in Union Square was painted in 1932. [p. 31] Bishop told me:

It was very important for me. I made it for my father. He had retired by then and had moved the family house to one in White Plains, so I

MR. BRO, c. 1935
Ink, 5 x 4 inches
Courtesy of Midtown Galleries, New York

TWO MEN IN UNION SQUARE, c. 1927
Etching, 7⅞ x 8¼ inches
Courtesy of Midtown Galleries, New York

made an "overmantle" for them. I used Union Square as a subject, crowds, people, the multiplicity of souls. I was reading Dante then, in a very literal translation. It struck me as a good story. It was the idea of the multiplicity of souls that was enormously important to me.

Now in the Delaware Art Museum in Wilmington, *Virgil and Dante in Union Square* hung for forty years in the home of Bishop's parents, loaned for exhibitions, but never put up for sale until the 1970s. It was a transitional work, struggling towards her more personal later statement, but still dependent upon the scaffolding of Miller's and Marsh's theories that had dominated her canvases of the late twenties. This was also the period of the 1930 painting *Union Square* [p. 31] and the etching of the same year, *On The Street* [p. 34].

But *Virgil and Dante in Union Square* soared beyond the vulgarizing tendency of these influences, not only in the brilliance of its graphic execution but also in its poetic ambiguity. If the multiplicity of human souls on the square are the sinners in a circle of hell, then hell is the ordinariness of daily living and the "sinners" face their "lives of quiet desperation" with a measure of patience, courage, and dignity that overlays the scene with a strange calm. There is a brilliantly lit, ar-

Isabel Bishop in Her Studio, c. 1950s

chitectural background in which disparate elements are used to fragment, overwhelm, menace, and finally to unite and uplift the alienated and indeterminate mass of people in the everyday costumes of the 1930s. Bishop's vision is particularized in the smallest of gestures: the stance of a figure, the slant of a hat brim, the drape of an article of clothing, the downward Zs of a fire escape, the mystical message of a commercial billboard mounted on the face of a building. An essentially artificial concept that might easily have resulted in the lameness of literary posturing, the *idea* of intermingling Virgil, Dante, and Union Square is enhanced by a mysterious and comforting beauty, not entirely explained by the skill of the painter in rendering the scene. It is foolish to speculate on the psychological underpinnings of a work of art, but the force in this remarkable work must surely arise in some measure from Isabel Bishop's felt emotional deprivation in her relationship with her mother and the profound nourishment the Union Square environment afforded her.

Nourishment was the actual word Bishop often used.

I didn't paint looking out of the window, but I placed my easel in such a way that I could look out and verify what I was doing. "Is it so?" I would ask myself and be able to look out to see if it was good, if it was saying the right thing. It was like eating, like nourishment, to look out and see people, going in all directions, a kind of ballet, very ornate. For a number of summers after my husband died, I taught in Skowhegan, Maine, and enjoyed it immensely, but when I would come back from Maine to the square, I'd feel afresh the miracle of this movement, the incredible richness of this coming and going of these multitudes of people. I can't fully explain, but it was like eating, looking out of my window on the people walking below, it was nourishment. I felt this movement as a totality, movement coming from so many different directions. I would keep turning my head to see the totality, the whole situation turning.

In 1934, Isabel Bishop married Harold George Wolff, a brilliant young doctor. She told me that she had been afraid of marriage, that she saw it as a potential threat.

Yasuo Kuniyoshi's first wife was a close friend, Katherine Schmidt, a very distinguished artist. She was very young when they married. She tried to do everything. They lived in Brooklyn Heights. She came into Manhattan every day to work in the lunchroom of the Art Students League. Katherine kept a meticulous house and did the rounds of the dealers with her husband's work, Kuniyoshi's work. All that while painting some of her own best pictures. I didn't know that I could function like that.

She invited the young doctor to dinner, impressing him with her adroitness in having prepared a festive meal on her tiny stove. "Actually I had sent out for the food, and never told him I hadn't cooked it myself."

Why had Bishop married then, given her apprehensions? She did not use the word love in her explanation. "Desperation" was the word she chose.

That's how it appeared to me at the time. What I felt was that it was a matter of having no choice as to how I would spend my life—as an artist. Marriage resolved the desperate difficulties. So, you see, I felt I had no other choice.

By 1934, she felt herself somewhat established as an artist. She had a signed contract with the Midtown Galleries and had been given her first solo exhibition. There was no question of her giving up a studio when she moved to her husband's Riverdale home and became the doctor's wife. "He didn't think a woman should have to give up her work when she became a wife. No, not at all. Nor when she became a mother either."

Isabel Bishop had married a most intriguing individual, a brilliantly talented neurologist, one

16

of the country's leading scientists, who was described by his colleagues as a formidably authoritarian and rigid personality. No hint of these traits appeared in Isabel Bishop's discussion of her marriage. She stressed her husband's passionate interest in music and the plastic arts, but, above all, she extolled his liberated attitude towards his wife's work.

At a time when the word "supportive" had not entered the vocabulary of men-women relationships, he was indeed very much so, intensely proud of her accomplishments and determined that her work continue without interference. Even after the birth of Remsen, their only child, a son born six years later in 1940, she told me how her husband had insisted that she return to her daily routine at her studio directly after the baby's birth.

It was very important that he took that attitude and it was very unusual for that time. We left the house together every morning; he went on to his work and I went to my studio. There was never any question about it.

A different picture emerges from more distant sources. Friends describe being entertained by the Wolffs as an extraordinary exercise in control over guests. Evenings were planned entirely by Dr. Wolff. Bishop was a gracious but subservient hostess, quite formally attired to match her husband's then outmoded formality of white flannels and blue blazer. A tray of drinks—Old Fashioneds or Manhattans or some such drink that nobody would have ordered—were set out, one for each guest. The program for the evening was rigidly designed. Free conversation during drinks. Silence during dinner, while recorded music by Mozart or Hindemith, chosen by their host, played. During coffee, a segment of discussion on a political, social, or artistic topic of the day, and so on, down to the exact hour guests were expected to leave.

Another report by a Riverdale neighbor added the detail that guests were handed three-by-five cards, neatly typed, listing the evening's agenda and its exact time schedule. Exaggerated or even apocryphal, the prevalence of such stories indicates a frightening degree of dominance.

Dr. Harold George Wolff fits the paradigm of an earlier generation's concept of the doctor as "great man." He was certainly one of the "great men" at New York Hospital when the reputation of a hospital was made by its innovative medical research men. He is remembered not only for his considerable accomplishments in the field of neurology and in the training of young promising doctors but also as a martinet, who was obsessive about punctuality and appearance and who made uncompromising demands on his subordinates for perfection in performance. Interns and residents

vied for his favor, longed for his approval, and feared his displeasure.

The circumstances of his death were equally dramatic. One of the country's foremost experts on brainwashing, he was summoned to Washington in February 1962 on the occasion of the exchange between the United States and the Soviet Union of the accused and convicted spies Colonel Abel and U2 pilot Gary Powers. Powers had just arrived in the country and was to be carefully examined and evaluated by Dr. Wolff, after his confession, trial, conviction, and imprisonment in the Soviet Union. The time had been set for very early morning. Dr. Wolff didn't appear at the precise hour. His rigid habits of punctuality were so well known that his team of medical experts was instantly alarmed. His hotel room door was unlocked, and Dr. Wolff was found in his bed, the victim of a fatal cerebral hemorrhage.

Impossible to project the impact on a marriage of such an overwhelming presence, Bishop herself makes no allusion to such possible strains on the relationship. She indicates household problems. Dr. Wolff's mother lived with them for the first fifteen years of the marriage. "She helped with Remsen, our son," Bishop told me. To my question, "Was that good?" she answered, "It was helpful. And it was difficult." Remsen's adolescence was apparently stormy. There was a period of alienation and ill-feeling between parents and son. But Remsen was very much a presence during my visits in 1987 at the Riverdale house where he was staying with his mother during her last illness. He is a photographer and her study proudly displayed samples of his artistry.

Bishop had been given her first solo exhibition in 1933. By 1940, she had had a number of shows at the Midtown as well as group exhibitions at the Art Students League, at the Whitney Museum of American Art, at the Virginia Museum of Fine Arts, and at the Golden Gate International Exposition, and she had collected the first of many prizes awarded to her through her life. She had been appointed an instructor at the Art Students League. Her 1935 oil *Two Girls* [p. 72] had been bought by the Metropolitan Museum of Art, where it now hangs in the Lila Acheson Wallace Wing of 20th-Century Art. In 1938, she executed a mural for a post office in New Lexington, Ohio, commissioned by Section of Fine Arts, U.S. Treasury Department, as part of the New Deal program for public art in America. In 1936, the art critic Emily Genauer in the *New York World Telegram* announced, "Isabel Bishop, we say with vehemence and conviction, is one of the most important woman painters in America today."

And, in 1937, a critic in *Scribner's* magazine declared, "It is safe to say that there is scarcely a woman painter in this country today to compare with her in the mastery of those elements that give a picture solidity and depth."

In 1940, the year of her son's birth, Bishop exhibited at the New York World's Fair, was awarded first prize in a show at the American Society of Graphic Artists, and was elected an Associate of the National Academy of Design in New York.

Dozens of honors followed. Year after year, museums purchased her works. In 1946, she was the first woman to be elected an officer of the National Institute of Arts and Letters since its founding in 1898. She was the recipient of a number of honorary degrees. In 1974, the Whitney Museum mounted a retrospective. In 1987, she received the Gold Medal for Painting of the American Academy and Institute of Arts and Letters. It cannot be said that Isabel Bishop was neglected.

She worked slowly, painstakingly. She told me:

An artist with the gift of spontaneous creation is very lucky. I didn't have it. I was always at the point of throwing the thing away. But then I would start again, going backwards and forwards on it and changing it and perhaps sawing down the panel and scraping it and all of that which would never be recommended as a method. For me it has been an unfortunate necessity. The way you say a thing is part of what you say, so you have to choose the right way. Method is a part of the aesthetic meaning of the painting.

The Bishop method was indeed a very complex one, beginning sometimes with on-the-spot sketching, followed by drawings, then by etchings and aquatints, all of which served as studies for the painting to come. "It bothers me when I am praised predominantly for drawings or prints, since for me, the end was the painting. All the rest was leading to the painting."

In an interview with Barbaralee Diamonstein in 1979 that appeared in *Inside New York's Art World*, Isabel Bishop discussed the importance of drawing and printing.

In order to come to an image that I could then work on in painting, I have to come at it . . . in complicated ways. You have a drawing, and a way of finding out if there's any what I call idea in the drawing—by idea, I mean a visual idea—is to make an etching, because an etching is a more austere medium. Then in recent years putting aquatint tone on that plate in order to arrive with a certain freedom at a tone that will be serendipitous. There is a lot of chance in aquatint. Your hand does something that maybe you wouldn't think of. Your hand does

17

something, and something can come out of that which results in an image, and I can really go after it in painting. It won't be the same thing, because it will be quite different in painting from what it was in black and white.[1]

Bishop used a laborious process of preparation for a painting. First, the masonite panel was treated with as many as eight coats of gesso, front and back. She borrowed a technique used by Rubens and painted a ground of random horizontal gray stripes made up of gelatin, powdered charcoal, and white lead, thus creating the transparent, vibrating surface she needed for her concept of figures in a weblike, mobile environment. The drawing was then added in pencil or ink and black or umber tempera. Then varnish was applied and blotted at once in order to keep the gesso less absorbent of the oil paint that was to be applied over it. Tone upon tone was then overlaid on this tacky ground, the striped underpainting remaining visible through the layers of oil. In some cases, to further balance light and shadow, Bishop applied fine random horizontal and vertical lines, that look almost like stitching, on the surface of the finished paintings. Enlarged photostats of the etchings, tacked to the easel, held Bishop to her original "metaphor," the visionary spark that had set the painting off in her mind.

"I do use a very complex technique I'm sorry to say. Not because I wanted to be complex, but in an effort to make the painting speak back to me. I'd do anything to get that result." In a long interview conducted in 1959 by M. B. Cowdrey, Warren Chappell, and Henrietta Moore, now in the files of the Archives of American Art, Bishop elaborated: "My trouble isn't in the technique. The trouble is my imagination works slower." In an almost Jamesian revelation, she vividly described the "germ," the "metaphor," for *Soda Fountain with Passersby*, 1960 [p. 121].

There is something very moving to me visually, and also in its meaning, in a lunch counter at the corner of Twenty-third Street and Fifth Avenue. The place is an open sort of plan in hot weather and enclosed with glass in cold weather. It has a fascinating, beautiful warmth and at the same time it's backed by mirrors which reflect the cool of the street and the outside world. Figures seem phantasmagorical in there as you look at the place from across the street because they're both reflected and seen directly. I love it, but I have to make the painting say what I feel about it. How? I don't know. I've been working on it for a couple of months. I've made endless small sketches, not, I'm afraid, with the aim of making the subject more literally right, but simply to keep the feeling that I have about it alive.

And in the same interview, in reference to the subway paintings of the late fifties, she described a similarly revealing urgency to "get it right." Talking about the fourth or fifth version of *Subway Scene*, 1958 [p. 119], an oil and tempera painting on gesso panel in the collection of the Whitney Museum of American Art, she said:

I think this finally has more of what I was aiming at. I was trying to express something that I feel aboout the subway and it isn't exactly what one is expected to see when one goes down there. It was very hard, especially as my experience had been only with figure painting and the figures in this are almost not discernible. This had to be so, because when I tried to . . . nail them down, the whole subject froze and none of the meaning that I wanted was present. I came to feel that . . . there had to be above all a non fixity in the situation . . . the subway can be so easily literally portrayed as a prison, which was not what I saw. I didn't know this until I began to create and I began and I drew it and I drew the uprights and so on, and it became a prison more and more. This isn't what I wanted or why I go down there and draw the place. It isn't to my mind a prison. So I got to see that the only way I could convey anything of my vision was to . . . hardly create the figures in trying to suggest their being kind of a map of life. It's there . . . in the appearing and disappearing in this situation that makes the charm of it for me.

It is interesting to compare Bishop's conception of the subway with other paintings having the same subject. Reginald Marsh's 1930 tempera painting *Subway Station* was certainly a strong influence, though perhaps more so on what Alloway calls the "deep frieze" technique used in *Soda Fountain with Passersby* and, particularly, in the later walking paintings. Paul Cadmus created his grotesque scene of a hellish place, *Subway Symphony*, in 1975, and, in 1950, George Tooker created a subway as the supreme metaphor of imprisonment and oppression of the human soul. In contrast, Bishop's subway is unique in its sense of movement. It transports the viewer. Her subway is a carrier, a means of flight, almost. The very architecture soars, delivering its workers and middle-class humanity to another dimension, suffused with the golden tones that the art historian Milton Brown described as Bishop's "transparent shadows and loaded lights." And how different in its basic concept is *Soda Fountain with Passersby*, compared to Edward Hopper's frozen tableau *Nighthawks*, with its evanescent mobility, its all-encompassing gossamer web linking exterior and interior, and its striking command of separated figures loosely and freely moving in a community of individual activity.

Subway Scene, 1958, makes connections to works of an earlier age by Piranesi and by Thomas Girtin and J. M. W. Turner. It evokes, within Bishop's philosophical spirit of a causal and continuous world, the grand aims of humanism. The arches connote a religious feeling, as does the iconography of the head reflected in the mirror of the vending machine. The transparency of the figures, the fleeting mobility of the human forms, enmeshed in physical space, reach outward to a real world—itself in infinite motion, a continuous web of space and time—that is, in Wordsworth's lines from *The Prelude*, "the very world which is the world / Of all of us, the place in which, in the end / We find our happiness, or not at all."

Bishop has been designated a realist. By the 1950s, the heartbreaking and violently damaging schism between the "realists" and the "abstract expressionists" was a fact of life in the art world. As in all wars, each contending side tells the story from a point of prejudice.

In the aesthetic war, the practitioners and advocates of abstract expressionism thought they had been ill-used and discriminated against during the reign of American realism and, particularly, during the New Deal period, when the WPA art projects were a potent force in keeping afloat more or less penniless artists. Public art did indeed favor figurative painters then, although a thin smattering of abstract artists made it into the post offices and public buildings. Realists, who never looked upon themselves as an exclusive school, insisted that they had been entirely eclectic, welcoming good art anywhere it showed up without any political or formal prejudice. The thirties and forties had also seen the establishment of artist's associations, founded in the spirit of the collegiality and shared problems of all artists, whatever their artistic differences: the American Abstract Artists, the American Artists' Congress, and the Artists' Union, among them. Organizations make for politics, unfortunately, and there were always dissenting artists who clearly felt leaned on and obstructed. The only instance, in our conversations, of Isabel Bishop talking badly of a fellow artist occurred when she told me of her extreme anger at Stuart Davis for pressuring her to "sign something or join some protest to do with the Artists' Union. I can't recall the details. He simply wouldn't take no for an answer, but kept on pressuring me. I didn't appreciate that. I didn't want any pressure from either side."

Certainly, the war was political as well as aesthetic. A democratic socialist upsurge of spirit that had been dominant in the thirties and forties collapsed in the 1950s. The Holocaust, Hiroshima, and atrocities perpetrated by Socialist societies on their own people took their toll on the dreamers of peace, plenty, and happiness for all. On any given day since 1950, half the world has been at the other half's throat, economically, politically, militarily, and aesthetically.

In their bitter rift, artists were echoing an ugly split that divided the entire country, but there was a special loss for those artists of Union Square and Fourteenth Street who witnessed their unique community splintered into competing fragments. In time, with the universal acceptance of abstract art, "realists," a term loose enough to cover any practitioner of figurative art, became almost non-persons, not even mentioned in the journals and art columns, a state which, for some artists associated with the primacy of realism, is still true today.

It is odd that Isabel Bishop, whose interests had never been political, became one of the founding members of *Reality*. Initiated by Raphael Soyer to stem the virtual tidal wave of abstract expressionism, the new journal was suggested as the organ for the expression of diverse opinions of realist artists.

Barbaralee Diamonstein, in an interview with Bishop in 1979, quotes her as saying:

The critics really went overboard. There was no discussion by any critical journal of anything but abstract expressionism. It took over the whole scene. I didn't happen to know Raphael Soyer . . . I had a card from him—this was about 1950—that said, "Tomorrow some artists are going to meet at this restaurant, called Del Pezzo, and would you like to come?" Well, I came and there was Ben Shahn, Soyer, Marsh, Kuniyoshi . . . no other woman at that point . . . Soyer wrote to a lot of painters because he thought it was a time when figurative painters should come together and talk. We adored it, loved it, and Del Pezzo put us out because we didn't drink enough.

Ben Shahn, who was then enormously famous, had just been through the country lecturing at universities, and he was shocked at what he found in the universities' art departments . . . the students didn't know anything . . . they were ignorant, they had no library of slides, they weren't taught any art history, they were just being disciplined in one mode—abstract expressionism—and they became very good at it, a great many of them . . . but they had no leverage on any change of style. They were just given this one way, they had no leverage for any changes. . . . We thought of what to do, and we thought we would like to at least express ourselves, so we got together a little paper, Reality. *I was totally opposed to its name, but no one listened to me.*

Jack Levine, who was one of the group,

wanted it to be called From the Horses's Mouth *which was just right, but it was called* Reality. *We got articles from Kokoschka, from Berenson, from a good many distinguished people abroad and a good many distinguished people here, and made quite a stir. In four years we issued four copies—four copies in four years—and these weren't sold, we sent them to universities and libraries and so on. Art magazines became absolutely furious. They wrote long diatribes . . . after four issues there was no use going on— we had all said what we had to say. But it is remembered now as a sort of collector's item.*[2]

Jack Levine remembers Isabel Bishop as the pluralist of the group. In a conversation over coffee, he described her position in the great quarrel as one of leadership through neutralization, negotiation, and diplomacy. Levine preferred a more aggressive attack. Militaristic terminology dotted his comments. The abstract expressionist group was "the Cedar Tavern Junta"; their "war" against figurative artists was "a hail of guided missiles" directed against an invented enemy, a war that pitted aesthetics against politics, the politics having been ascribed to the "realists" and the aesthetic concerns claimed as the exclusive concern of the abstractionists. Levine sees the reign of the abstract expressionists as leading to the present state of the arts, in which painting, "like the dress business," is ruled by questions of money, profit, and the latest fashionable cut.

Bishop's involvement in *Reality* sprang from a deep commitment to the idea of image. "It is part of the artist's business to push toward an image," she said. "You have to fight for it. A new image, symbolic of its period, in the way we say a Roman head or an eighteenth-century man." There was a period when Bishop thought it would be abstract expressionism that would break through to this new image. She pointed to de Kooning's pink women canvasses as one of the new possibilities, but she came to believe that the energy and hope of the abstractionists was dissipated and finally lost in pop art.

She remained open, generous, and catholic in her judgments. Leonard Baskin, who served on a number of art juries with her, told me that he too found her conciliatory and overly pluralistic. "She liked everything," he said. "Down to the junk." Laughing, she told me, "Baskin and I disagreed about everything, every single thing, except that we each admired one another's work."

Her work has always been widely admired by other artists. She proudly recounted that de Kooning was reported to have said, "That woman's nudes are the best damn nudes ever." The many honors she received, the retrospective exhibitions,

Isabel Bishop with Models, c. 1958. Courtesy of Midtown Galleries, New York

and the museum purchases of her work are a testament to the respect the art community paid her work. Even critics transcended their own bias against figurative art to praise Bishop. In the September/October 1975 issue of *Art in America* Lawrence Alloway, in an attempt to fill a gap in the vision of his generation of critics, inadvertently reveals the depth of the bias:

Isabel Bishop is not as securely a part of recent art history as she ought to be. She still suffers from the fact that for many of us American painting begins with Abstract Expressionism, and artists who precede it, even when individually attractive, are considered premature. But the Abstract Expressionists no longer constitute a wall between ourselves and earlier American art, just as they no longer have the power to confine our attention to abstract art above other forms. There are critics for whom Bishop has been present and honored all along, but I am not one of them, so I have to speak in terms of recovery.

But Alloway's act of recovery in this article culminates in another limitation set by a critic. Bypassing much of her work, he emphasizes what he calls Bishop's "vivid sense of intrasexual contact and affinity. The world can be said to enter her art to the extent that she deals with woman as subject matter, singly or in groups." And Alloway goes on to stress that her most distinctive works are those in which two women appear. "She needs two people as her subject, and, for whatever reason, they have to be women. Without that she cannot depict the web of mutual responsiveness which is at the core of her meaning and which is rarely found in the history of the painting of couples."

"By comparison," he continues, "her infrequent paintings of male and female couples are less sharply observed and more sentimental. Male figures on their own, such as in her early paintings of bums, are generalized and blunt compared to her studies of women. The bums look like fumbled Daumier figures."

On the subject of Bishop's nudes, Alloway reports the puzzlingly self-conscious declaration Bishop reiterated in interviews. "I have no sexual interest in females." He goes on to say of these paintings that they are "handsomely done, with a touching sense of humanness . . . they do not, however, match her pictures of women together." Amazingly, he makes no mention whatever of the self-portraits. Perhaps they weren't known to him.

One can agree with Alloway on the very special quality of her pictures of women in pairs, without praising her at the expense of the rest of her work. Isabel Bishop's considerable contribution to the art of our time is manifested in the totality of her output. This is not enormous, considering the length of her life and her lifelong commitment to art. She worked slowly. There were years in which she did only two to four paintings, and the scale of her work was small, apart from the mural in the Lexington Post Office and a three-panel screen at the Art Students League. Her largest oil painting, *Virgil and Dante in Union Square*, measures only 27 by 52 inches; and it is always a shock, given the power of its lasting impact, to see that the shimmering beauty, the psychological depth, and the subtle interplay of feeling in *Two Girls* is framed in a space of 20 by 24 inches.

Oversize splash and the flagrant color of much

modernist painting was not within her aim or her interest. "Color is not the original motif for me. My fundamentals are form, space, and light." She told me that she tacked to her easel certain strips of fabric against which she tested her colors; and she kept on hand illustrations of Chinese ceramics in a copy of R. L. Hudson's *Chinese Art* to test relationships between her color schemes and the celadons and misty blues of Ming dynasty porcelains. Such tentativeness might indicate a problem in her use of color. There are limitations in the range of Bishop's palette, but, within the aesthetic rules she sets herself, a rare and distinctive surface is perfected in which her aim of projecting figures in a seamless web is wonderfully realized. By using underlayers and stripes of misty gray—almost white—then overlays of scumbled yellow, umber, bluish-gray, and a burst of orange, an opaque and transparent illusion is created within which Bishop's solid, particularized yet anonymous forms are given the mobility she desired.

A highly articulate and literate artist, Bishop acknowledged the traditions and mentors that influenced her: among others, Peter Paul Rubens, Kenneth Hayes Miller, Reginald Marsh, Adolf van Hildebrand's theories in *The Problem of Form in Painting and Sculpture*, and Paul Tillich's essay on seeing, quoted in part, below:

We never see only what we see; we always see something else with it and through it! . . . If we look at a human face, we see lines and shades, but with it and through it we see a unique, incomparable personality whose expressions are visible in his face, whose character and destiny have left traces which we un-

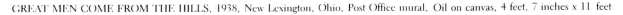

GREAT MEN COME FROM THE HILLS, 1938, New Lexington, Ohio, Post Office mural, Oil on canvas, 4 feet, 7 inches x 11 feet

derstand and in which we can even read something of his future. With and through colors and forms and movements we see friendliness and coldness, hostility and devotion, anger and love, sadness and joy. We see infinitely more than we see when we look into a human face.[3]

It is the magic of this "infinitely more" that occurs in Bishop paintings. Couples have never been painted with such tender intimacy and revelation. The mysterious interaction of feeling in human community has seldom been attempted at all; in Bishop's work, it is beautifully consummated. A 1943 oil on gesso panel, *Resting* [p. 93], portrays a man and woman, both asleep in a public place, the waiting room of a train station, or riding a train or a bus, perhaps. Their surroundings, never spelled out, only suggest this interpretation. The woman leans on her own arm, the man's head droops on her shoulder. She wears an odd little, off-the-face hat, very much of the period, as is the felt-brimmed hat on her companion's lap in the foreground. In the mutual exhaustion of this lower-middle-class couple and in the reversal of their roles—the woman supporting the man's resting head, rather than the other way around—physical and emotional tenderness and trust is expressed without any sentimentality or cuteness.

A retrospective of Bishop's work, mounted at Loyola Marymount University, was titled "The Affectionate Eye." Affectionate seems the wrong word for Bishop, a term more suited to Norman Rockwell. Bishop's eye is piercingly loving, "the eye of a novelist," as John Russell has said, the eye of a good novelist, not one looking merely for charm and anecdote but for universal meaning and depth, which is unerringly revealed in Bishop's work.

Not that Bishop eschewed charm. The painting had to speak to her in profound terms: "Is it so?" But all her considerable technique was commanded to make how it was so, exquisite. As early as 1934, she struggled with facial gesture to depict the psyche underneath, even exploring grotesquely mundane gestures, as in *Tidying Up* [p. 91], *Toothache*, *Blemish*, *Girl with Frankfurter* [p. 114], *Blowing Smoke Rings* [p. 90], and in the etching *Laughing Head*. "It's very difficult to paint a smile," she said and worked at it in etchings and drawings such as *Laughing Girl*, 1934 [p. 74], until the preparation culminated in the exquisite painting *Young Woman's Head*, 1937 [p. 67], which told her, "It is so."

Bishop put great stress on theories of mobility that served to satisfy the aesthetic and social effects she reached for. One of her great gifts, the sense of movement in her figures, was stretched by her

BLEMISH, 1945
Oil on gesso panel
21¾ x 15¾ inches
Private collection

LAUGHING GIRL, 1936
Etching, 4¼ x 3¼ inches
Courtesy of Midtown Galleries, New York

TOOTHACHE, 1949
Oil and tempera on canvas
12 x 9 inches
Whereabouts unknown

LAUGHING HEAD, 1934
Oil on gesso panel
13 x 12 inches
The Butler Institute of American Art
Youngstown, Ohio

Preliminary drawing of Mr. Darcy and
  Elizabeth for *Pride and Prejudice*, 1945
Ink and ink wash, 11 x 8¼ inches
Private collection

"She affectionately embraced her"
Illustration for *Pride and Prejudice*, 1945
Ink and ink wash, 11 x 8¼
The Pierpont Morgan Library, New York

in her writings to become a metaphor of the possibility for social mobility in her subjects. For me, this is a false note, but fortunately it is struck only in her theorizing and kept out of the actual paintings. Condescension is totally absent in her paintings of working girls. There is no hint of the self-congratulatory attitude of a "correct" social stance, of the artist raising the subjects above themselves, of endowing them with qualities granted by the artist, qualities too elevated to be found in these sitters in nature. She does not exhort us to see a patina of virtue artificially affixed by the artist, nor the swagger of monumentality, such as that imposed by Marsh when he was not satirizing. She looks closely at a section of life and discovers simplicity and beauty.

In *Girls Sitting in Union Square Fountain*, 1936 [p. 80], a painting that served as the study for the exquisite oil and tempera on gesso panel *Two Girls with a Book*, 1938 [p. 81], Bishop explained that she was trying

for an effect of lightness and casualness, both in the subject and the modeling . . . the arbitrary shadows and lights connecting the figures of the girls and fountain were meant to suggest a general interplay between the little figures and their environment . . . the motive was really the weaving together of the forms of the fountain and the children, in the effort to express a certain charm I felt in the children's relation to their world.

In the painting, the background has been abandoned for the more profound interrelationship between the two figures. The two girls command and fill the space, building an intimacy between them and the book in a pattern of loving enclosure, their hunched bodies and the position of their hands and arms almost balletic in their mirror likeness. Only the outdoor clothing of the two figures hints at a background of park or public space, although the viewer places them there unerringly. One is reminded of Hemingway's admonition to himself to know everything there was to know

about his characters and their story, but to throw most of that away before beginning to write.

Bishop herself was most eloquent on this topic. Sometime in the forties, she was commissioned to illustrate a new edition of Jane Austen's *Pride and Prejudice*. For reasons having to do with postwar paper shortages and the shortage of metal for plates, publication was delayed until 1976. (The thirty-one pen-and-ink drawings are at The Pierpont Morgan Library. It is interesting, given Alloway's emphasis, that the most enchanting of the group is of two women embracing: Elizabeth and Jane, in a balletlike movement of intertwined arms and clothing, accented and connected by Bishop's thin black nervous line at hem, waist, and floating sash, the whole a triumph of mobility, contact, and feeling.) At the time of publication, she wrote an afterword, part of which is quoted below:

My involvement in this undertaking has to do also with my feeling . . . that in Jane Austen's handling of the writer's problem, certain . . . factors relate . . . to my own efforts as an artist over fifty years. . . . She doesn't describe, in detail, environments; while she gives you the immediate social context of her characters, she is silent about the wider context (you don't know the general economic situation, or that England was at war); she doesn't allow you to care what people had on, or even about the details of their physiognomies! She governs the questions you are allowed to ask—she forbids any impulse to ask others. . . . What she presents to you as important convinces you utterly, in its completeness . . . and assumes monumentality . . . she limits her esthetic problem and . . . gains great power through it. What a lesson for visual art! In fact, the whole "modern" period of painting (since 1910) has been preoccupied with some aspect of this problem.[4]

Once again in eloquently voicing her admiration for another, she defines herself and her elegant, powerful, lasting presence for the art of our century.

BIBLIOGRAPHY

Bishop, Isabel. *Reginald Marsh: Etchings, Engravings, Lithographs*. New York: Frederick A. Praeger, 1956.

Fine, Elsa Honig. *Women and Art*. Montclair/London: Allanheld and Schram/Prior, 1978.

Harris, Ann Sutherland and Nochlin, Linda. *Women Artists—1550–1950*. New York: Los Angeles County Museum of Art/Alfred A. Knopf, 1976.

Lunde, Karl. *Isabel Bishop*. New York: Harry N. Abrams, 1975.

Marqusee, Janet. *Painting America: Mural Art in the New Deal Era*. New York: Midtown Galleries, 1988.

Munro, Eleanor. *Originals: American Women Artists*. New York: Simon and Schuster, 1979.

Park, Marlene and Markowitz, Gerald E. *Post Offices and Public Art in the New Deal*. Philadelphia: Temple University Press, 1985.

Reich, Sheldon. *Isabel Bishop*. Tucson: The University of Arizona Museum of Art, 1974.

Rubenstein, Charlotte Streifer. *American Women Artists*. New York: Avon Books, 1982.

St. John, Bruce. *Isabel Bishop: The Affectionate Eye*. Los Angeles: Laband Art Gallery, Loyola Marymount University, 1985.

Teller, Susan Pirpiris. *The Artists of Union Square*. New York: Associated American Artists, 1987.

———*Isabel Bishop: Etchings and Aquatints*. New York: Associated American Artists, 1985.

———*The WPA Guide to New York City*. New York: Pantheon Books, 1982.

NOTES

[1] Barbaralee Diamonstein, *Inside New York's Art World* (New York: Rizzoli International Publications, Inc., 1980), p. 35; reprinted by permission of the author.

[2] Ibid. p. 41.

[3] Paul Tillich, *The New Being* (New York: Charles Scribners Sons, 1955), p. 129.

[4] Jane Austen, illustrations and afterword by Isabel Bishop, *Pride and Prejudice* (New York: E. P. Dutton, 1976), p. 415.

THE EARLY WORK

I took my work under my arm, and went around to the galleries. The Midtown Galleries were being formed by a young man just out of Harvard. He was looking around for people, and I just took my work in to show to him. And he took it. . . . That was very important to me. Like other young people, I'd been sending things in to national jury shows, sending and sending and sending. They came back many times, and once in a while something stuck, and that was very encouraging.

I remember sending two of the dark pictures I was painting—anything but in style—[to the Pennsylvania Academy of Art]. One was of Union Square—arbitrary and dark with quite a lot of little figures in it—and the second was a still life of my painting table, which was a very dull picture with a lot of bottles on it. And they both got in, to my absolute amazement.

I was trying everything very hard. I was very miserable. Frustrated. One tries, and it doesn't [work]—one "blows in" one way and it comes out another way. In the end it isn't at all what one wanted. And yet, whatever validity can be found in one's work has to be found there, in what one didn't consciously or deliberately intend.[1]

—ISABEL BISHOP

THE BROKEN TEACUP #2, 1927
Oil on canvas, 17 x 14 inches
Courtesy of Midtown Galleries, New York

STILL LIFE WITH ORANGES #2, c. 1928
Oil on canvas
25¼ x 30 inches
Courtesy of Midtown Galleries, New York

(opposite above)

STILL LIFE WITH BOTTLES, 1931
Oil on canvas
25 x 37 inches
Edwin A. Ulrich Museum of Art
The Wichita State University, Wichita, Kansas
Endowment Association Art Collection

THE WICKER CHAIR, c. 1929
Oil on canvas
19⅞ x 17 inches
Courtesy of Midtown Galleries, New York

(opposite below)

ARTIST'S TABLE, 1931
Oil on canvas
14⅝ x 17½ inches
National Museum of American Art
Smithsonian Institution, Washington, D.C.
Gift of the Sara Roby Foundation

Studies for VIRGIL AND DANTE IN UNION SQUARE, 1932
Pencil, 6¼ x 3¼ inches
Courtesy of Midtown Galleries, New York

Untitled, c. 1930
Pencil, 9¼ x 6½ inches
Collection of Elsa and Stanley Sidel

(above)
VIRGIL AND DANTE IN UNION SQUARE, 1932
Pencil, 13 x 26 inches
Palmer Museum of Art, The Pennsylvania State University
University Park

(below)
Studies of Union Square, c. 1932
Pencil, 3 x 8½ inches
Courtesy of Midtown Galleries, New York

(opposite above)

VIRGIL AND DANTE IN UNION SQUARE, 1932
Oil on canvas
27 x 52 inches
Delaware Art Museum, Wilmington

UNION SQUARE, 1932
Oil on canvas
14 x 17¾ inches
Nebraska Art Association
Nellie Cochrane Woods Memorial Collection
Courtesy of Sheldon Memorial Art Gallery
University of Nebraska-Lincoln

FIFTEENTH STREET AND SIXTH AVENUE, 1930
Oil and tempera on gesso panel
17 x 14 inches
Courtesy of Midtown Galleries, New York

HEARN DEPARTMENT STORE—FOURTEENTH STREET SHOPPERS, 1927
Oil on canvas
10 x 12 inches
Private collection

UNION SQUARE, 1930
Oil on canvas
16 x 20 inches
Courtesy of Midtown Galleries, New York

BOOT BLACK, 1933–34
Oil on paper mounted on fiber board, 19⅞ x 17 inches
Hirshhorn Museum and Sculpture Garden, Smithsonian Institution, Washington, D.C.
Gift of Joseph M. Hirshhorn, 1966

I suppose that one's first experience is very, very forming. So, that long time with drawing made me feel . . . that drawing was kind of rock-bottom for me, and I have to keep very close to it. I suppose that's the reason I make so many, many drawings for every painting. And etching has got to seem to me a way of testing a drawing idea. Perhaps you have two figures, or you have a figure and a building, or something of that sort, and you want to find out for yourself whether it is an idea, whether there is a visual idea in there, a nucleus that you could develop. And if you make that an etching, which is a more austere medium than pen drawing, you find out whether there is or isn't such a nucleus there. Then I find that I can work on the thing forever, you see—that nucleus will make it possible, even though it will never be a successful painting. It is possible always to evolve it, to find certain relationships in it, even if one can never bring it off. . . . And then, etching is a lovely change from painting. It's so different. There's so much process to it. If you're in a dry period, the process is lovely. You like to clean the plates for hours and put the grounds on. There's so much of that sort of thing—a little like cooking, or something like that![2]

—ISABEL BISHOP

ON THE STREET (FOURTEENTH STREET), 1931, Etching, 4¹⁵/₁₆ x 10¹³/₁₆ inches, Collection of Whitney Museum of American Art, New York

(*opposite above*) Study for AT THE BASE OF THE FLAGPOLE or IDLE CONVERSATION, 1928
Pencil, 5 x 6 inches
Courtesy of Midtown Galleries, New York

(*opposite middle*) Study for AT THE BASE OF THE FLAGPOLE or IDLE CONVERSATION, 1928
Pencil, 5¼ x 7¾ inches
Collection of Mr. Edward Ripling

(*opposite below*) AT THE BASE OF THE FLAGPOLE or IDLE CONVERSATION, 1928
Etching, 5 x 6 inches
Collection of Mrs. Walter Fillin

CONVERSATION, 1931
Etching, 6 x 4 inches
Collection of Dr. Jacob J. Vargish

SPECTATORS, 1933
Etching, 7 x 5 inches
Courtesy of Midtown Galleries, New York

WAITING, 1930
Etching, 6 x 3⅞ inches
Collection of Mrs. Walter Fillin

(opposite)
STUDIES FOR GREAT MEN CAME FROM THE HILLS
(mural) 1938 [p. 20]

ON THE STREET (FOURTEENTH STREET), 1932
Oil on canvas
14½ x 26 inches
Private collection

Ink and gouache
8¼ x 21¼ inches

Ink and gouache
8 x 21½ inches

Ink and gouache
8¼ x 21¼ inches

SELF-PORTRAITS

I hope my work is recognizable as being by a woman, though I certainly would never deliberately make it feminine in any way, in subject or treatment. But if I speak in a voice which is my own, it's bound to be the voice of a woman.[3]
—ISABEL BISHOP

I think it's something perhaps that has to be justified—making one's motif out of gestures. If you think of work that has put so much value on that aspect, I suppose you'd think of genre painting. In this case, you'd think of the little Dutchmen who did this, but, of course, in a superlative way, so that you might say there was no reason to try this again, ever. But on the other hand, our life is entirely different, and it gives one a feeling of exploration to try to find some gestures that are characteristic of our life.[4]
—ISABEL BISHOP

(left)
SELF-PORTRAIT, c. 1928
Ink and oil, 6 x 4½ inches
Private collection of Mr. and Mrs. Floyd T. Amsden

(right)
SELF-PORTRAIT, c. 1927
Pencil, 7 x 4½ inches
Collection of Ms. Betty Beer

SELF-PORTRAIT, 1927, Oil on canvas, 14 x 13 inches, Edwin A. Ulrich Museum of Art, The Wichita State University, Wichita, Kansas, Endowment Association Art Collection

(opposite above left)
SELF-PORTRAIT #2, 1927
Oil on canvas
19 x 16 inches
Courtesy of Midtown Galleries, New York

(opposite above right)
SELF-PORTRAIT, 1928
Oil on canvas
18 x 14 inches
Uffizi Portrait Gallery, Florence, Italy

(opposite below right)
SELF-PORTRAIT, 1928
Oil on canvas
20 x 16 inches
Collection of Anthony Mitchell

(opposite below left)
SELF-PORTRAIT CARICATURE, c. 1930
Pastel on paper, 14 x 12 inches
The Heckscher Museum, Huntington,
    New York

(right)
SELF-PORTRAIT #1, c. 1927
Oil on canvas
18 x 14 inches
Courtesy of Midtown Galleries, New York

SELF-PORTRAIT, 1984
Oil on gesso panel
16¼ x 13 inches
Private collection

SELF-PORTRAIT, 1985–86
Oil on gesso panel
17⅞ x 13⅞ inches
Collection of Dr. and Mrs. Thomas Bagnoli

(opposite)

SELF-PORTRAIT, 1986
Oil and pencil on gesso panel
20 x 15¼ inches
Collection of Mr. and Mrs. McCauley Conner

41

NUDES

I find the most nourishing thing of all, to start one off again, is to get somebody to take their clothes off and then to draw from the nude.[5]

—ISABEL BISHOP

A shape, like a word, has innumerable associations that vibrate in the memory and any attempt to explain it by a single analogy is as futile as the translation of a poem. But the fact that we can base our argument either way on this unexpected union of sex and geometry is a proof of how deeply the concept of the nude is linked with our most elementary notions of order and design.[6]

—ISABEL BISHOP

(left)
NUDE (back view), 1925
Etching, 6⅝ x 5⅝ inches
Collection of Mrs. Walter Fillin

(below)
NUDE (front view), 1925
Etching, 10 x 6⅞ inches
Collection of Mrs. Walter Fillin

NUDE BY STREAM, 1938
Oil and tempera on gesso panel
26 x 20 inches
Private collection

(*opposite*)

NUDE IN INTERIOR, 1947
Oil and tempera on canvas
21 x 18 inches
New Britain Museum of American Art
New Britain, Connecticut, Stephen Lawrence Fund

NUDE, 1934
Oil on gesso panel
33 x 40 inches
Whitney Museum of American Art, New York

NUDE, 1938
Ink and wash, 5¾ x 6½ inches
Collection of Edward Jacobsen

Study for NUDE IN INTERIOR, c. 1947
Ink, 14 x 10⅜ inches
Whitney Museum of American Art
Bequest of Felicia Meyer Marsh

NUDE BENDING, 1949
Oil and tempera on canvas
21 x 24 inches
Collection of Mr. Russell Cantlay

48

NUDE BENDING, 1949
Ink and ink wash, 5¾ x 5½ inches
Private collection

Study for NUDE BENDING, 1949
Ink, 5 x 6 inches
Courtesy of Midtown Galleries, New York

NUDE #2, 1954
Oil and tempera on gesso panel
31 x 21 inches
Des Moines Art Center, Des Moines, Iowa
Rose F. Rosenfield Purchase Fund, 1958

NUDE, c. 1955
Oil and tempera on gesso panel
17¾ x 20¾ inches
University of Arizona Museum of Art, Tucson
Gift of C. Leonard Pfeiffer

(opposite)
UNDRESSING, 1959
Oil and tempera on gesso panel
28 × 24½ inches
Altanta University, Atlanta, Georgia

NUDE, RISING FROM BED, c. 1936
Ink, 6¾ x 4¼ inches
Courtesy of Midtown Galleries, New York

THE PEDICURE, c. 1970
Ink and ink wash, 9½ x 6¼ inches
Private collection

53

NUDE REACHING, 1964
Oil and tempera on canvas
28 x 35 inches
Indianapolis Museum of Art, Indianapolis, Indiana
Gift of the National Academy of Design

(opposite above)

WOMAN UNDRESSING, 1961
Oil and tempera on gesso panel
21 x 35 inches
Collection of Sue and David Workman

(opposite below)

STUDY FOR UNDRESSING ON THE BED, 1960
Graphite, oil, and tempera on canvas
19 x 28 inches
Bayly Art Museum of the University
  of Virginia, Charlottesville

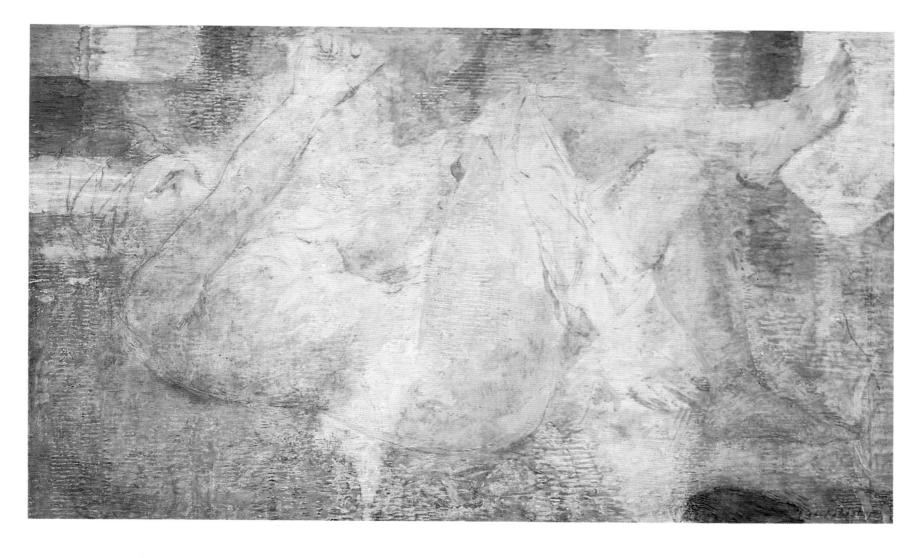

NUDE SKETCH, 1975
Oil on gesso panel, 12 x 15 inches
Private collection

NUDE HOLDING FOOT, 1969
Pen and ink, 5¾ x 8¼ inches
Collection of Dr. and Mrs. Margolis

UNDRESSING ON THE BED, 1960
Ink wash, 4½ x 8 inches
Courtesy of Midtown Galleries, New York

RECUMBENT NUDE, c. 1960
Ink wash, 5 x 10½ inches
Courtesy of Midtown Galleries, New York

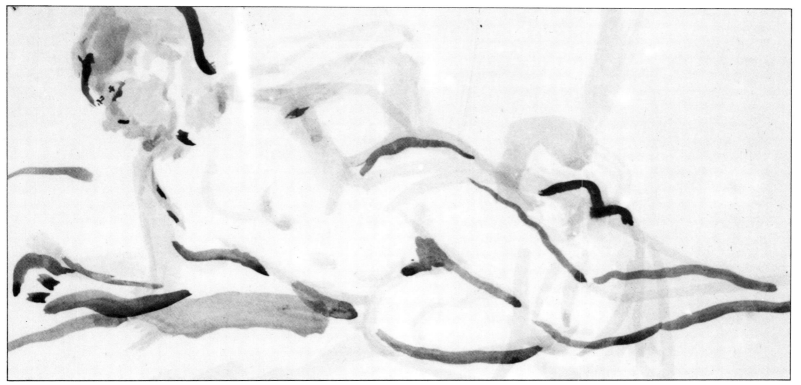

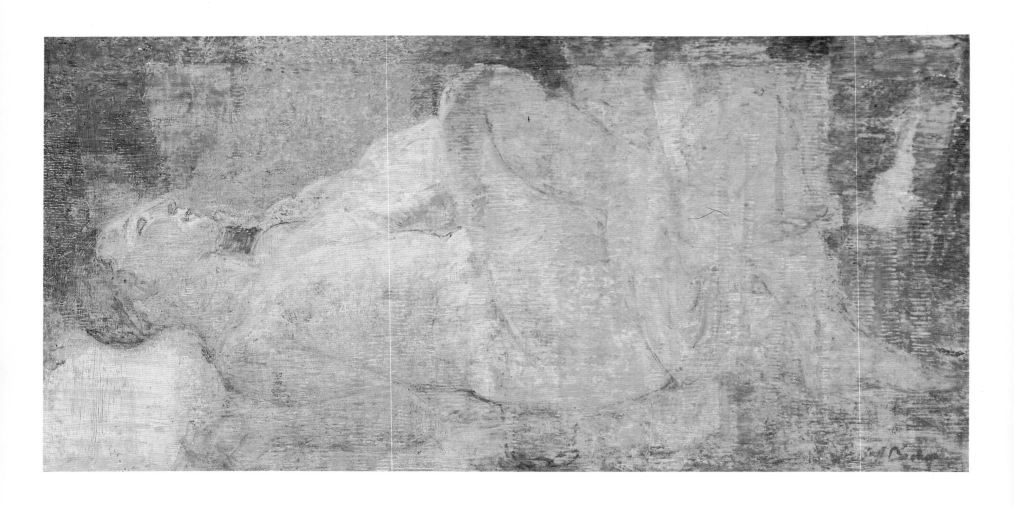

UNDRESSING ON THE BED, 1960
Oil and tempera on gesso panel
18½ x 37 inches
Courtesy of Midtown Galleries, New York

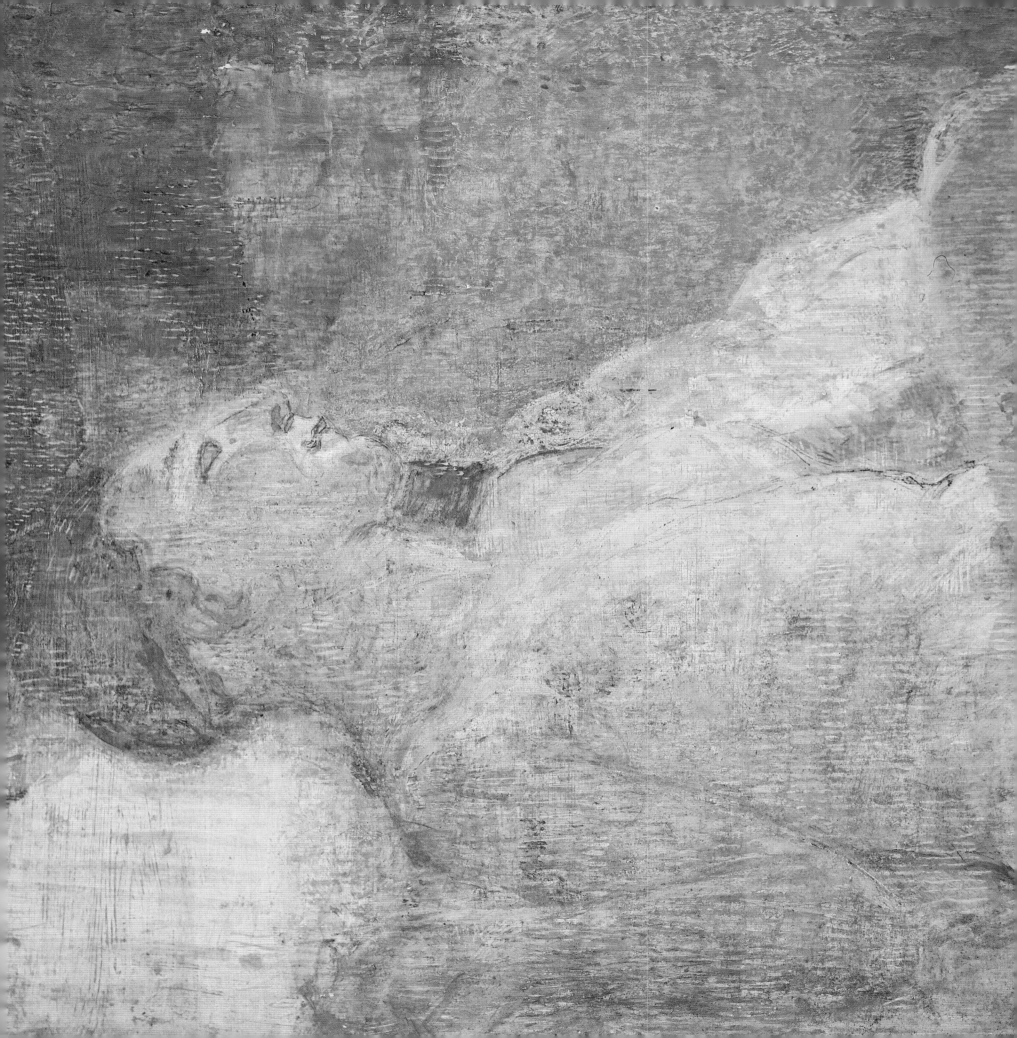

SMALL NUDE, 1943
Oil on gesso panel, 15 x 13¾ inches
Private collection

(opposite)

PREPARATION, 1944
Oil and tempera on canvas
22 x 20 inches
The Marjorie and Charles Benton Collection

(opposite)

WOMAN UNDRESSING, c. 1945
Ink and ink wash, 8 x 8 inches
Courtesy of Midtown Galleries, New York

(right)

Study for UNDRESSING ON THE BED, 1961
Etching and aquatint, 3½ x 6 inches
Courtesy of Midtown Galleries, New York

(below right)

LITTLE NUDE, 1964
Etching and aquatint, 5¾ x 5 inches
Courtesy of Midtown Galleries, New York

(below left)

SEATED NUDE, c. 1964
Ink wash, 5¼ x 3½ inches
Courtesy of Midtown Galleries, New York

62

64   SEATED NUDE, 1967, Oil and tempera on gesso panel, 23½ x 21 inches, Collection of Mr. and Mrs. John Wierdsma

LITTLE NUDE, 1965, Oil and tempera on gesso panel, 27 x 22 inches, Collection of Sue and David Workman

THE PEOPLE OF UNION SQUARE

Union Square interests me in a way that I don't understand myself. I think it has to do with a deep association from the time of my childhood, when my family lived one street from the "good" neighborhood in Detroit, and there was a kind of appetite that I developed for the other direction, toward the slum region. It seemed warmer to me. It seemed more human, and I liked it better. . . . I feel that may be part of the reason for my loving the Union Square area, which is a rather shabby business region of New York. Yet young women that one sees here strike me as having a rather rich connotation. Of course, they're young—the ones that I'm thinking of are young—and they don't live in this region, as I know, because I've corraled some of them and got them into my studio. They generally live in the Bronx and work here. It's a moment in their lives when they are really in motion, because they, of course, are looking for husbands and, at the same time, they're earning their living. . . . The time that I try to catch them, that I'm interested in trying to present, is when they are in their lunch hour, the hour of respite, when both these things seem to me to be communicated—that is, their double purpose. I catch them, I feel, in a moment during the day when they have stopped but, in a sense, the work day is continuing. . . . I don't know, there may be deep reasons why I should be so much interested in eating, but it seems to me an activity that has a great deal of meaning for human beings, as it does for other animals.[7]

—ISABEL BISHOP

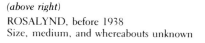

(above right)
ROSALYND, before 1938
Size, medium, and whereabouts unknown

(right)
HEAD OF A YOUNG GIRL, 1939
Oil and tempera on gesso panel
17 x 14 inches
Whereabouts unknown

YOUNG WOMAN'S HEAD, c. 1937
Oil and tempera on gesso panel
20 x 17 inches
Whereabouts unknown

COMBING HER HAIR, 1932
Egg tempera and oil on wood panel
20 x 17 inches
Collection of Dr. and Mrs. John E. Larkin, Jr.

FEMALE HEAD, c. 1935
Oil on canvas
12 x 10 inches
Whitney Museum of American Art, New York
Shmidt Shubert Bequest

THE KID, 1936
Oil on gesso panel
20 x 17 inches
Whereabouts unknown

Study for TWO GIRLS, 1935
Ink and ink wash, 3¼ x 4½ inches
Collection of Richard Wagner

TWO GIRLS, c. 1935
Gouache, 17 x 23 inches
The Butler Institute of American Art,
      Youngstown, Ohio

TWO GIRLS, 1935
Oil and tempera on gesso panel
20 x 24 inches
The Metropolitan Museum of Art, New York
Arthur Hoppock Hearn Fund, 1936

(opposite)

GIRL IN NEW YORK (HEAD #2), 1938
Oil and tempera on gesso panel
20 x 16 inches
Colorado Springs Fine Arts Center
Colorado Springs, Colorado

Five Studies for LAUGHING HEAD, 1934
Ink and ink wash; 6½ x 10 inches
Collection of Michael Robinson

(below)
LAUGHING HEAD, 1934
Etching, 4⅞ x 3⅞ inches
Collection of Mrs. Walter Fillin

(right)
WOMAN AND BOY ON A BENCH, 1935
Ink and ink wash, 5½ x 7 inches
The Trenton Museum, Trenton, New Jersey

WAITING, 1938
Oil and tempera on gesso panel
19⅞ x 15⅛ inches
Wadsworth Atheneum, Hartford, Connecticut
Bequest of Anne Parrish Titzell

DELAYED DEPARTURE, 1935
Etching, 6⅞ x 5¾ inches
Collection of Mrs. Walter Fillin

*Very few artists use models anymore. They work from the imagi-
nation. The limitation that I have to accept at present is the need
for this person that will seem real to me and that I can feel is
connected with the kind of environment that I'm presenting.*[8]
—ISABEL BISHOP

THE CLUB, 1935
Oil and tempera on canvas
20 x 24 inches
Collection of Mr. and Mrs. Edwin H. Wegman

(opposite)

WAITING, 1938
Oil and tempera on gesso panel
29 x 22¼ inches
The Newark Museum, Newark, New Jersey
Arthur F. Egner Memorial Fund Purchase, 1944

GROUP OF MEN, c. 1935
Ink and graphite, 4¼ x 3½ inches
Wadsworth Atheneum, Hartford, Connecticut
Gift of Henry Schnakenberg

(below)
MEN AT UNION SQUARE
  (page from a sketchbook), 1936
Pen and ink, 5 x 7½ inches
Collection of Dr. Jacob J. Vargish

THE WHISPER, c. 1938
Ink and ink wash, 3¾ x 3½ inches
Collection of Dr. and Mrs. Alfred Nodel

(below left)

SHOWING THE SNAPSHOT, 1936
Etching, 4 x 3 inches
Collection of Mrs. Walter Fillin

GIRLS SITTING IN UNION SQUARE FOUNTAIN, 1936
Etching, 5⅞ x 4⅞ inches
Courtesy of Midtown Galleries, New York

GIRLS SITTING IN UNION SQUARE FOUNTAIN, 1936
Oil and tempera on gesso panel
16 x 14 inches
Courtesy of Midtown Galleries, New York

TWO GIRLS WITH A BOOK, 1938
Oil and tempera on gesso panel
20 x 24 inches
Private collection

STOOPING MAN, 1936
Oil and tempera on gesso panel
12 x 10 inches
Private collection

(left)
Study for NOON HOUR #1, 1935
Ink, 9½ x 6 inches
Private collection

(left)
NOON HOUR, 1935
Etching, 6⅞ x 4⅞ inches
Courtesy of Midtown Galleries, New York

(above)
Studies of Two Girls, c. 1935
Ink and ink wash, 12½ x 7 inches
Collection of Elsa and Stanley Sidel

83

AT THE NOON HOUR, 1939
Oil and tempera on gesso panel
25 x 18 inches
Museum of Fine Arts, Springfield, Massachusetts
The James Philip Gray Collection

84

LUNCH HOUR, 1939
Oil and tempera on gesso panel
27 x 17½ inches
Collection of Mrs. Alan D. Gruskin

YOUNG WOMAN, 1937
Oil and tempera on canvas
30 x 21¼ inches
The Pennsylvania Academy of the Fine Arts, Philadelphia
Gilpin Fund Purchase

OFFICE GIRLS, 1939
Oil on gesso panel
28 x 18 inches
Private collection

TWO GIRLS OUTDOORS, 1946
Oil on gesso panel
30 x 18 inches
The Corcoran Gallery of Art, Washington, D.C.
Museum Purchase, Anna E. Clark Fund, 1945

LUNCH COUNTER, 1940
Oil and tempera on gesso panel
20 x 15 inches
The Phillips Collection, Washington, D.C.

ENCOUNTER, 1940
Oil and tempera on gesso panel
24 x 16 inches
The Saint Louis Art Museum, Saint Louis, Missouri
Eliza McMillan Fund

ICE CREAM CONES, 1942
Oil and tempera on gesso panel
34 x 20 inches
Museum of Fine Arts, Boston
Charles Henry Hayden Fund

BLOWING SMOKE RINGS, 1938
Oil on gesso panel
15 x 12 inches
Collection of Mrs. Jean Howard

90

TIDYING UP, 1941
Oil on gesso panel
15 x 11½ inches
Indianpolis, Museum of Art, Indianapolis, Indiana
Purchased from the Delavan Smith Fund

STRAP HANGERS, 1943
Oil and tempera on gesso panel
20 x 16 inches
Private collection

RESTING, 1943
Oil on gesso panel
16 x 17 inches
Private collection

PREOCCUPIED, 1953
Oil on gesso panel
10⅝ x 12¾ inches
Wadsworth Atheneum, Hartford, Connecticut
Bequest of Anne Parish Titzell

DOUBLE DATE DELAYED #2, 1948
Oil and tempera on gesso panel
19 x 15½ inches
Collection of Mr. and Mrs. Gerry Gariepy

YOUNG SMOKERS OUTDOORS
Medium, size, and whereabouts unknown

96

(opposite)
DOUBLE DATE DELAYED #1, 1948
Oil and tempera on gesso panel
22³⁄₁₆ x 18³⁄₁₆ inches
Munson-Williams-Proctor Institute Museum of Art
Utica, New York

MENDING, 1945
Oil on gesso panel
25 x 16½ inches
National Museum of American Art
Smithsonian Institution, Washington, D.C.
Gift of S. C. Johnson & Son, Inc.

SEATED MAN, c. 1956
Ink wash, 6½ x 5 inches
Collection of Paul Anbinder

I found that if you have one person come in from the square . . . then it's rather easy to get others. It's hard to get the first one. They're frightened, they won't come, they suspect you. But after one man came, I had a series of cronies of his. They're interesting. They pose very well. I should think that they'd be very self-conscious and stiff, but they seem to sense what you want them for, what you've brought them in for, and so they act as themselves. They behave as they behave in the park.[9]

—ISABEL BISHOP

(below left)

SOLITAIRE, 1936
Ink, 4¼ x 5 inches
Private collection

THE ASH CAN, c. 1935
Ink and ink wash, 5¾ x 4½ inches
Courtesy of Midtown Galleries, New York

GIRL READING NEWSPAPER
(GIRL WITH A NEWSPAPER), 1946
Oil on canvas
29 x 18 inches
The Nelson-Atkins Museum of Art
Kansas City, Missouri

FRIENDS, 1946
Oil and tempera on gesso panel
17 x 11½ inches
Collection of B. J. Stebman

THE COAT, 1941
Oil and tempera on gesso panel
15½ x 10½ inches
Courtesy of Dorsky Gallery, New York

DRINKING FOUNTAIN, 1947
Oil and tempera on gesso panel
14½ x 11½ inches
Private collection

(above)

THE FOUNTAIN, 1947
Ink, 4⅛ x 3⅛ inches
Private collection

(right)

MAN AT A DRINKING FOUNTAIN, c. 1950
Pen and ink, 3⅝ x 4¼ inches
Courtesy of Midtown Galleries, New York

(below)

Two studies for DRINKING FOUNTAIN, 1947
Ink, 10½ x 4½ inches
Courtesy of Midtown Galleries, New York

TWO GIRLS AT LUNCH STAND, 1956
Ink and ink wash, 8½ x 6¼ inches
Collection of Dr. Jacob J. Vargish

WOMAN WITH HOT DOG, c. 1945
Ink and ink wash, 9½ x 4½ inches
Private collection

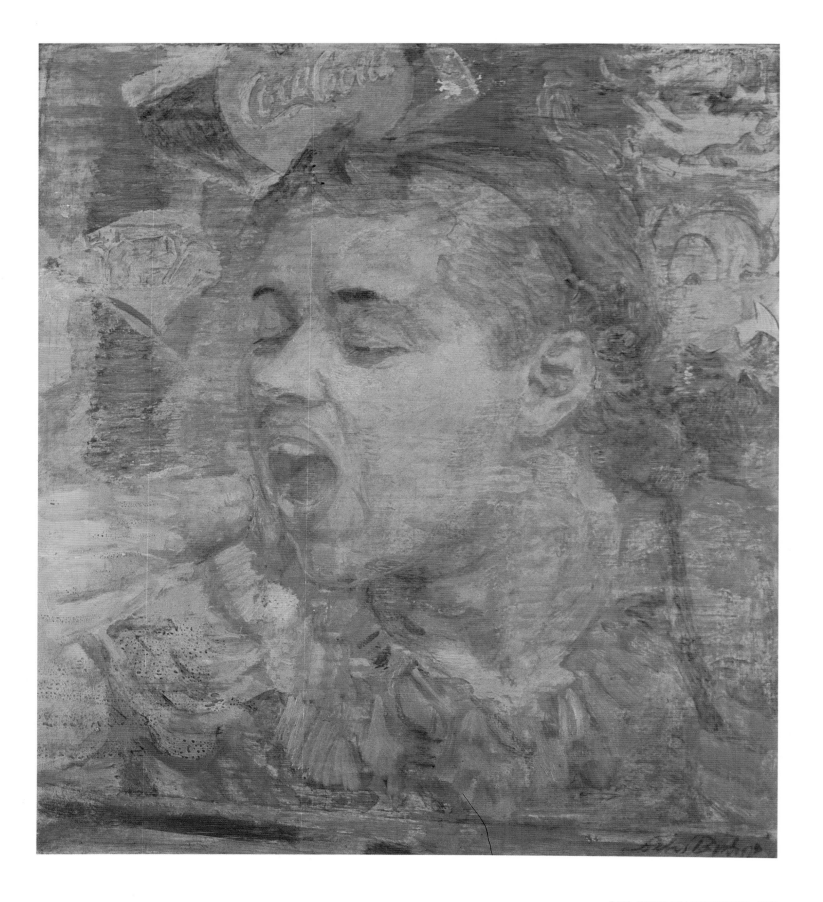

GIRL WITH FRANKFURTER, 1945
Oil on gesso panel
14 x 12½ inches
Collection of Harold William Brown

104

INTERLUDE, 1952
Oil and tempera on gesso panel
32 x 20 inches
Collection of Mrs. Alexander D. Falck

GIRLS IN THE SUBWAY STATION, 1953
Oil and tempera on gesso panel
32 x 20 inches
Collection of Dr. B. B. Berle

PUTTING ON THE JACKET, c. 1943
Ink, 6¼ x 5½ inches
Courtesy of Midtown Galleries, New York

TWO WITH JACKETS, 1949
Ink and pencil, 8⅜ x 4⅜ inches
Courtesy of Midtown Galleries, New York

THE APRON, c. 1937
Medium, size, and whereabouts unknown

REACHING FOR THE COAT, 1943
Etching, 5⅞ x 4 inches
Courtesy of Midtown Galleries, New York

PUTTING ON THE COAT, 1943
Etching, 5⅞ x 3⅞ inches
Courtesy of Midtown Galleries, New York

THE COATS, 1967
Oil, tempera, pencil, and ink on canvas
31 x 33 inches
The Brooklyn Museum, Brooklyn, New York
Gift of Mr. and Mrs. Robert E. Blum

THE COATS, 1966
Etching and aquatint, 7½ x 7⅞ inches
Courtesy of Midtown Galleries, New York

PUTTING ON THE COAT, c. 1965
Ink wash, 7 x 4½ inches
Courtesy of Midtown Galleries, New York

THE COATS (counterproof), 1966
Etching and aquatint, 7½ x 7⅞ inches
Courtesy of Midtown Galleries, New York

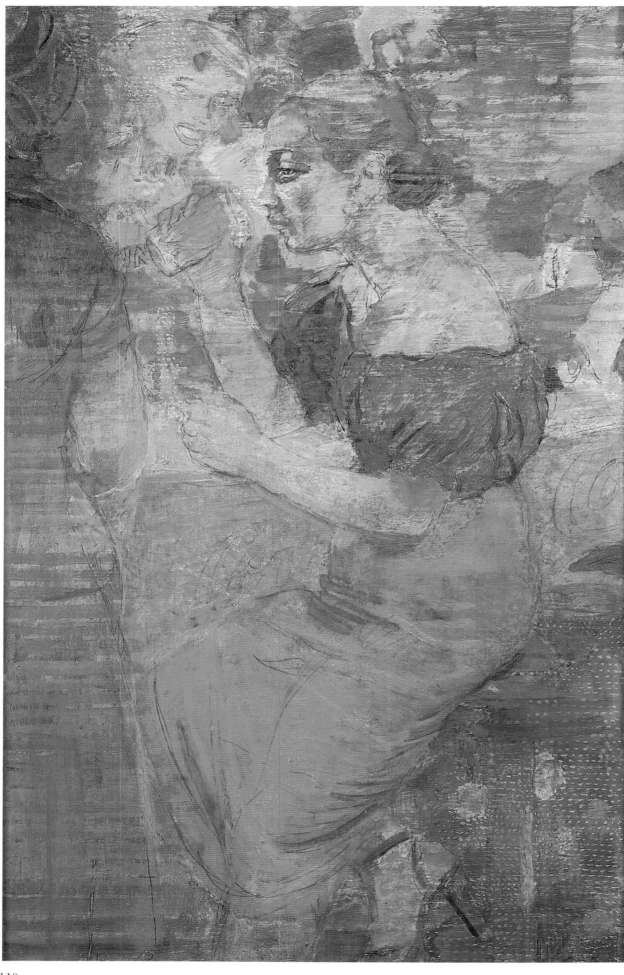

OUT TO LUNCH, 1953
Oil on canvas
24¼ x 16¼ inches
Collection of Dr. Jacob V. Vargish

(opposite)

SNACK BAR, 1954
Oil on gesso panel
13½ x 11⅛ inches
Columbus Museum of Art, Columbus, Ohio
Museum Purchase, Howald Fund

(above left)
AT THE FOUNTAIN, c. 1957
Ink wash, 8 x 5 inches
Courtesy of Midtown Galleries, New York

(left)
SNACK BAR, 1959
Etching, 6⅞ x 4⅜ inches
Courtesy of Midtown Galleries, New York

Study for AT THE COUNTER, c. 1952
Oil and tempera on gesso panel
25⅞ x 17¾ inches
Private collection

TWO STRAP HANGERS (Study for CONVERSATION), 1955
Ink wash, 7⅞ x 5⅞ inches
Private collection

(above right)

STRAP HANGERS, c. 1938
Ink wash, 10 x 5 inches
Courtesy of Midtown Galleries, New York

(right)

STRAP HANGERS, 1940
Etching, 6⅞ x 4 inches
Courtesy of Midtown Galleries, New York

(opposite)
HOMEWARD, 1951
Oil and tempera on gesso panel
26 x 20 inches
Courtesy of Midtown Galleries, New York

SUBWAY READING, 1956
Oil and tempera on gesso panel
24½ x 17¾ inches
Private collection

Study for STRAP HANGERS, 1943
Pencil, ink, and ink wash, 9 x 4 inches
Private collection

Studies for STRAP HANGERS, c. 1940
Pencil, ink, and ink wash, 14⅜ x 13¾ inches
Courtesy of Midtown Galleries, New York

Study for SUBWAY SCENE, 1956
Charcoal, 23 x 14½ inches
Courtesy of Midtown Galleries, New York

Study for SUBWAY SCENE, 1956
Oil and charcoal on canvas, 38½ x 27¼ inches
Courtesy of Midtown Galleries, New York

117

UNDER UNION SQUARE, 1957
Oil and tempera on gesso panel
40 x 28 inches
Collection of Dr. John C. Weber

STUDY FOR SUBWAY SCENE, 1957–58
Oil on canvas
40 x 28 inches
Courtesy of Midtown Galleries, New York

SUBWAY SCENE, 1957–58
Oil and tempera on gesso panel
40 x 28 inches
Whitney Museum of American Art, New York

THE WALKING PICTURES

I have come to think that walking is absolutely beautiful, and I could not tell you why.[10]

—ISABEL BISHOP

I had taken some time away from New York and had been in Maine where I had been taking the greatest pleasure in the wide open stretches of the beach in the early morning, with perhaps one or two figures there, and in the sky so high and so beautiful. This was in my consciousness when I stepped off the train at Grand Central Station and came out [at] Park Avenue and Forty-second Street, and I was struck by the beauty, drama, and miraculous effects of a crowd of people in motion. It seemed magical. It seemed as though the movement involved more than I could take in with my eyes because the air became solid—it was like a continuum, this ambience in which this beautiful interchange took place. I felt inspired to try something that I felt and do feel, that perhaps artists have not ever tried because they didn't think it was interesting. . . . I don't know of anyone that I think has really wanted to do this. That is, to make this happen in some way on a canvas or a panel so that the spectators will believe that this isn't just described movement but movement taking place.[11]

—ISABEL BISHOP

FIVE WOMEN WALKING, 1968
Ink wash, 8⅜ x 10⅝ inches
Courtesy of Midtown Galleries, New York

STUDY FOR SODA FOUNTAIN
WITH PASSERSBY 1960
Oil and tempera on canvas
13¼ x 23⅜ inches
Collection of Mr. and Mrs. Richard E. Blum

SODA FOUNTAIN WITH PASSERSBY, 1960
Oil and tempera on canvas
24 x 36 inches
Virginia Museum of Fine Arts, Richmond
The John Barton Payne Foundation

FIVE WOMEN WALKING, 1967
Etching and aquatint, 7⅝ x 9⅞ inches
Courtesy of Midtown Galleries, New York

(below left)

Study for WOMEN WALKING IN SUBWAY STATION, 1963
Ink and ink wash, 8¼ x 10½ inches
Courtesy of Midtown Galleries, New York

(below right)

WOMEN WALKING IN THE SUBWAY STATION, 1963
Etching and aquatint, 8¼ x 6 inches
Collection of Mrs. Walter Fillin

Study for FIVE WOMEN WALKING, 1967
Ink wash, 8⅜ x 10⅝ inches
Collection of Mr. and Mrs. Howard Rosenberg

THREE STUDIES OF WOMEN WALKING, c. 1963
Ink wash, 8½ x 19 inches
Courtesy of Midtown Galleries, New York

FIVE WOMEN WALKING, 1967
Oil and tempera on gesso panel
31½ x 39½ inches
Private collection

FIVE WOMEN WALKING #2, 1967
Oil and tempera on gesso panel
31½ x 39½ inches
Edwin A. Ulrich Museum of Art
The Wichita State University, Wichita, Kansas
Endowment Association Art Collection

YOUNG PEOPLE #2, 1972
Oil and tempera on gesso panel
36 x 25⅝ inches
Montclair Art Museum, Montclair, New Jersey

126

SEVEN STUDENTS (early state counterproof), 1981–82
Etching, ink wash, and graphite, 6¾ x 8½ inches
Courtesy of Midtown Galleries, New York

SEVEN STUDENTS (early state), 1981–82
Etching, aquatint, and graphite, 6¾ x 8½ inches
Courtesy of Midtown Galleries, New York

WALKING, 1970
Oil and tempera on canvas
32 x 40 inches
Oklahoma Art Center, Oklahoma City, Oklahoma
Museum Purchase, Beaux Arts Society Fund

MEN AND GIRLS WALKING, 1970
Oil and tempera on gesso board
28½ x 39½ inches
Mount Holyoke College
South Hadley, Massachusetts

(left)
THREE SCHOOL GIRLS, c. 1974
Ink and ink wash, 6¼ x 7½ inches
Collection of Midtown Galleries, New York

(right)
OPPOSITE DIRECTIONS (unfinished), 1972
Etching, aquatint, ink wash, and pencil
8 x 5¾ inches
Whereabouts unknown

(below)
STUDENTS WALKING or SIX STUDENTS
   (first state), 1976
Etching, 8⅛ x 13⅝ inches
Courtesy of Midtown Galleries, New York

SCHOOL GIRLS, 1974
Etching and aquatint, 9¼ x 13 inches
Collection of Mrs. Walter Fillin

Study for SCHOOL GIRLS, 1974
Ink and ink wash, 8½ x 13½ inches
Courtesy of Midtown Galleries, New York

RECESS #3, 1976
Oil on gesso panel
31½ x 45¼ inches
Private collection

RECESS #2, 1975
Oil on gesso panel
31 x 44⅞ inches
Courtesy of Midtown Galleries, New York

CAMPUS STUDENTS #1, 1972
Oil and tempera on gesso panel
22½ x 40 inches
Private collection

THREE WALKING STUDIES, c. 1977
Pen, ink, and ink wash, 12 x 11 inches
Courtesy of Midtown Galleries, New York

TWO FIGURES, c. 1977
Ink, 7½ x 8½ inches
Courtesy of Midtown Galleries, New York

Study for HIGH SCHOOL STUDENTS, c. 1975
Ink, 7 x 5¾ inches
Courtesy of Midtown Galleries, New York

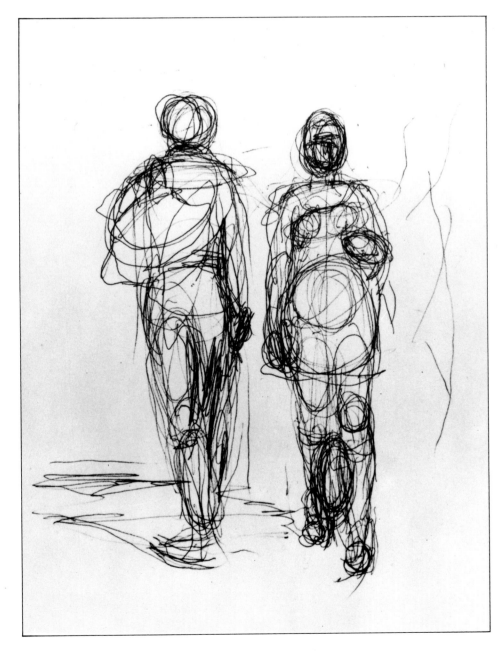

(opposite above)
STUDENTS WALKING OUTDOORS #2, 1978
Oil on canvas
25 x 44 inches
Courtesy of Midtown Galleries, New York

HIGH SCHOOL STUDENTS #3, 1974
Oil on gesso panel
25 x 40 inches
Collection of Sue and David Workman

(opposite below)
SUBWAY STATION UNDER GRAND CENTRAL #1, 1967
Oil and tempera on gesso panel
27 x 46 inches
Courtesy of Rosenfeld Fine Arts, New York

GIRLS AT COUNTER, 1982
Etching and aquatint, 6 x 5 inches
Courtesy of Midtown Galleries, New York

GIRLS AT COUNTER, 1982
Oil on canvas
32 x 22½ inches
Collection of Robert N. Taxin, D.O.

Study for ENTRANCE TO UNION SQUARE, c. 1980
Ink and ink wash, 12 x 8½ inches
Courtesy of Midtown Galleries, New York

YOUNG GROUP, UNION SQUARE ENTRANCE, c. 1980
Pen and ink wash, 6½ x 5½ inches
Courtesy of Midtown Galleries, New York

CAMPUS STUDENTS #2, 1972
Oil and tempera on gesso panel
34 x 38½ inches
Courtesy of Midtown Galleries, New York

(opposite)

STUDENTS, ENTRANCE TO UNION SQUARE, 1980
Oil on canvas
30 x 28½ inches
Courtesy of Midtown Galleries, New York

143

SOURCES FOR
ISABEL BISHOP QUOTATIONS
FROM PAGE 24 TO PAGE 120

1. From unpublished interviews with Isabel Bishop conducted in September 1957 by Louis M. Starr of the Oral History Research Office, Columbia University, New York, made possible by a grant from the Carnegie Foundation.

2. Ibid.

3. From unpublished interviews with Isabel Bishop conducted in 1978 by Patricia Depew for the film *Isabel Bishop: Portrait of an Artist*, distributed by Films Inc., Chicago, Illinois.

4. Ibid.

5. From Louis M. Starr interviews.

6. Cindy Nemser, "Conversation with Isabel Bishop," *Feminist Art Journal*, 1 (Spring 1976).

7. From Louis M. Starr interviews.

8. Ibid.

9. Ibid.

10. From Patricia Depew interviews.

11. Ibid.

(above)
VARIATIONS ON THE THEME OF WALKING, 1979
Oil on canvas
22¼ x 33¼ inches
Courtesy of Dorsky Gallery, New York

(below)
YOUTHS #3, c. 1980
Oil on gesso panel
24¾ x 44 inches
Courtesy of Midtown Galleries, New York

ISABEL BISHOP—
FIRST IMPRESSIONS

The grand, the heroic draftsmen . . . had better be the models [for artists], though one's aim be far from heroic or grand. With their august help one might learn to lay one's traps and spread one's nets, to snare the subject matter of one's own intuition and life experience, however small and special.[1]

———Isabel Bishop

Drawings have not traditionally found an appreciative audience in the United States. They are, by their very nature, contradictory to the American character. Whereas art that seems expressive of our native values is large, public, blatant, and rational, drawings are traditionally small, intimate, subtle, and intuitive. As such they frustrate the American desire for universal and instantaneous apprehension. Demanding a sensitive eye and a trained sensibility, drawings deny the egalitarian nature of our democratic ideals. Furthermore, drawings are identified by the public with the initial preparatory stages of a work of art and, therefore, have rarely earned the stature of painting or sculpture. In fact, in 1923 when the first serious book on drawings was published in the United States, Theodore Bolton's *Early American Portrait Draughtsmen in Crayons*, Bishop had already devoted several years to studying drawing with Kenneth Hayes Miller at the Art Students League in New York. It was there that she was tutored in the academic approach—drawing as a discipline and a preparatory procedure for painting. Although Bishop soon came to reject many of the lessons she was taught at the League, her early training there established a dedication to drawing that was to continue throughout her life. Her approach was dogged, her output prodigious. Drawing, she said, nourished her spirit., "it was like eating."[2]

Bishop's tireless devotion to excellence and the variety of her skills are evidence that the standards she took as her own were those established by the masters of pen, pencil, and brush the world over. Bishop was as likely to aspire to a seventeenth-century draftsman's command of these media as she was to that of an Eastern calligrapher's. She absorbed the vast history of drawing and applied its most formidable standards to the world she saw before her. Bishop's mastery of technical skills combined with a keen sense of observation enabled her to create a body of work that simultaneously documents an era and confirms the expressive power of pure line. This merging of the universal standards of draftsmanship with the visual particularities of her time and place define Isabel Bishop's major contribution to American art.

Nevertheless, Bishop always considered drawings to be preparatory stages of creativity, not as ends in themselves. In the methodical course that she established early in her career, drawings preceded prints, which ultimately were transformed into paintings. She devoted equal care to each step, an arduous procedure allowing her to complete as few as one or two, but rarely more than four paintings in an entire year of daily effort.

Thus a question arises regarding the public presentation of her drawings: If a drawing was intended only as a method of capturing an impression and of solving technical and compositional problems, is it a violation of its purpose to exhibit it as a finished work of art?

The answer to this question is suggested by the fact that Bishop signed each drawing, an indication of the importance she herself attached to these drawings as legitimate works of art. And, although themes were attempted over and over again, the drawings that resulted far exceed the mere recording of the evolution of an idea or the original impulse that was later refined and elaborated in a painting. They transcend mere likeness by conveying the entire range of tone, balance, and surface richness that is found in Bishop's paintings. The drawings yield the full opportunity for interpretation; they offer the complete measure of effort, skill, and intensity. Indeed, Bishop never progressed to the print stage until the drawing's potential had been fulfilled, just as no painting was undertaken until the print had earned the full measure of excellence.

Although Bishop's drawing style was remarkably varied, ranging from suggestive to dramatic, delicate to vigorous, deliberate to spontaneous, there is a consistent richness of means that is applicable even to those drawings which were the result of an instantaneous gesture, for that gesture was a summation of the trials and rehearsals that prepared her for the critical creative act. The history of each drawing is implicit in its refinement. Similarly, a drawing only a few inches in dimension displays Bishop's mastery of the full vocabulary of means. Lines broaden to convey weight and narrow to a thread to capture light. Long and meandering arabesques are used intermittently with jagged scribbles, each mark carrying a triple set of functions that at once renders the contour of the subject, the atmosphere surrounding the subject, and the tempo of the scene depicted. This graphic virtuosity was not summoned merely to create an accurate or even beautiful image. Bishop's goal was more challenging and more elusive. Not content to freeze a perfect image, she strove to give it life. And life, she believed, was conveyed through movement. Bishop's goal was to defy the static actuality of a drawing, that of lines frozen on a flat surface, in order to capture the essential qualities of life—suppleness, mood, and change.

In devoting herself to this elusive goal, it was necessary for Bishop to reject the lessons she had so diligently learned as a student. Years later, she described rediscovering paintings she had done as a student in Kenneth Hayes Miller's class at the Arts Students League.

I slashed them! Why they were terrible! Now, they were done . . . with the utmost earnestness, and I worked on those things and I worked on them, and they were finished, finished things. [But] they were completely off track.[3]

The artists Miller established as models for his students strove to produce the solidity of classical sculpture. Miller emulated Renaissance techniques, reviving methods developed in the early part of the fifteenth century that first rendered broad forms, drawn with clarity, which were then imbued with surface detail. Drawings made in this manner have a cold fixity that was antipathetic to the warmth and suppleness that Bishop wished to evoke. In a resolute manner, she set about her life's work in quiet protest against this academic style.

Bishop's work can be divided into four distinct periods: the controlled renderings of her student illustrations in the 1920s, the nervous line drawings of the 1930s, the full-tone ink gouaches of the 1940s and 1950s, and the atmospheric walking figures of the 1960s and 1970s. Yet each phase marked a stage in a steady progression toward her self-stated goal. It is instructive to isolate the means Bishop developed over the course of her life to create the unique quality of "aliveness" that distinguishes her work. Each technique was designed to convince the viewer that the subjects depicted had the ability to move naturally through space. Often, this movement was implicit. Figures seated and at rest conveyed movement as a potential state. But the depiction of people putting on coats, yawning, walking, chatting, and drinking added a narrative requisite to this task. Her challenge was to present the figure as a verb—active, transitive, evolving. No depicted moment was arrested; it was perpetually in the process of occurring.

Line is the primary tool for communication in almost all drawing. For Bishop, it had to be used to convey the impression of forms that would forever appear as alive as the model they were describing. Although Miller had taught her to use line to circumscribe the contour of a figure, Bishop discovered that this technique isolated the figure from the ground against which it stood, apparently freezing it in space and time. Consequently, she rejected this use of line in favor of more delicate modes of delineation, designed to dissolve contour. Some lines were allowed to disperse into broad strokes, thereby merging with the background, while others narrowed into threads, some even disappearing completely as they greeted the source of illumination. In this way, the feeling of light and air and space replaced the impression of solidity and weight. A scale of gradation of lights and darks was established that infused her drawings with an extraordinary range of atmospheric effects. Indeed, various bottles of diluted ink were available in her studio to provide a dozen different gradations of gray, each calculated to establish the subject in a shifting and dynamic world.

Along with the suppression of contour lines, Bishop tended to de-emphasize surface detail. Highlights and shadows were her major concern because these enhanced the freedom of the figure. Surface effects, such as patterns, colors, and textures, on the other hand, which are kinds of information that can be discerned only under circumstances of slow and intense scrutiny, were of less concern to her for they convey the impression that the subject is inert, denying rather than affirming the dynamic quality of life that was primary to Bishop's art.

For the same reason, Bishop rejected the Renaissance conventions for evoking three-dimensional space on a two-dimensional surface. She believed that the Renaissance techniques of foreshortening and of single-point projections locked figures within a rigid illusional space, contradicting lifelike mobility. Rather than adopt the logic of geometric space, Bishop chose an alternative, espoused in a book entitled *The Problem of Form in Painting and Sculpture*, published first in 1893 and reissued in 1945. Its author, Adolph van Hildebrand, according to Bishop,

> [felt] that the image which is flat is of the utmost importance in the perception of space. This must be strong, then the space is read from that image back, and that isn't exactly like a box-like space.[4]

Bishop further developed Hildebrand's theory by replacing single-point perspective with a process of integrating multiple points of view. This technique is particularly apparent in the walking figure series that occupied Bishop throughout the 1960s and 1970s. Although this method probably evolved as she grew older and had difficulty working outside her studio, it also clearly represents the development and extension of Hildebrand's theories of depicted space. In each of these "walking" paintings, several drawings are combined. Individual figures, which ultimately became integrated into a single work of art, were first approached as independent problems to be solved. Each was observed and recorded frontally in its own shallow space before being assigned a place within a larger composition. These compositions, therefore, were not taken from life; they were invented by the artist on the paper, plate, or canvas. In fact, in several works from this period, the same model reappears in a single composition, each appearance presenting a different pose or gesture. This approach is consistent with Hildebrand's theory:

> To perceive in visual terms the third dimension . . . we must imagine ourselves as changing our point of view, and as getting merely a succession of disconnected shifting views on the object more or less in profile.[5]

Finally, the kinesthetic potential of these figures was assured by substituting geometric space for atmospheric space. Bishop stated that her goal was to express that

> *potential [for motion] by visual means. . . . You can't describe it in words, it has to be expressed in the modeling. To express it in the modeling there has to be created in the onlooker . . . a sense of physical continuity, as by a subtle and delicate web throughout the picture.*[6]

This physical continuity was most apparent in Bishop's later work. In these drawings, her pursuit of a unified surface took the form of a denial of both the solidity of matter and the emptiness of space. Figures are suffused with atmosphere. At the same time the air becomes palpable.

Bishop stated that the air must be as positive as the figures who move through it.[7] In this way the individuals become integrated with the environment and the magical illusion of movement—and life—is achieved.

Bishop is explicit that it is the movement of the figures which fascinates her, not their relationships or personalities: "That they don't know each other is necessary to what I am fascinated with."[8] It is their coming together and their moving apart—like dancers in a ballet—that she wanted to capture.

The issue of content is problematic and invites comparison with other artists of her generation, particularly those who, like Bishop, retained their loyalty to the figure despite the gradual dominance of abstract art. Bishop never shared their tendency to utilize art as a propaganda tool. For many artists of her generation, art provided an opportunity to vent social indignation and to awaken political conscience. Perhaps it is due to the fact that her own life was comfortable and secure that Bishop seemed oblivious to the deprivation of others. The world she presented consisted exclusively of charming, fugitive instants. These she pursued until their most pleasing aspects had been intercepted for all time. Despite the fact that wars, political strife, and economic catastrophes were battering the nation throughout her most active years, Bishop never deviated in her delight in people as they existed on the domestic scale—combing their hair, sipping soda, and putting on their coats. Life's little moments were sufficient to satisfy Bishop's lifelong artistic purpose—to capture living forms moving through space and light.

The artists of Bishop's generation who concentrated on figuration evoked cynicism and social protest (Ben Shahn, George Grosz, Ivan Albright, Käthe Kollwitz, William Gropper). Those who shared her dynamic world view tended to represent dynamism in terms of machines, war, and technology (Joseph Stella, Lyonel Feininger, Charles Sheeler). If the city was the subject, it was portrayed as a lonely or fearsome place (Edward Hopper, John Marin). In contrast to all of these tendencies, Bishop's city is a place of orderly and unthreatening activity, and its inhabitants seem perfectly adapted to it. Even the bums, who frequently served as models, appear to have accepted their fate in good spirit.

The artists who presented the ordinary aspects of American life (Reginald Marsh, Edward Hopper, Yasuo Kuniyoshi, Raphael Soyer, Philip Evergood, Edwin Dickinson, and Milton Avery) all developed distinctive ways of portraying anonymous people going about their daily business or enjoying simple pleasures. These are the same subjects that captivated Isabel Bishop, but it is only in Isabel Bishop's work that the great seventeenth-century Dutch and Flemish tradition of the masters of genre, such as Rembrandt and Adriaen Brouwer, is clearly evident. Like them, Bishop chose prosaic subjects to record in a humble, uncritical manner. Like them, she eschewed technical flourishes and superfluous gestures. Likewise, despite the fact that subjects were never idealized, they were depicted in such a refined manner that even a sketch qualified as a mode of artistic expression in its own right.

Consistent with the tradition of genre art, Bishop rejected art "in the grand manner"[9] and insisted that its means and purposes exclude the visualization of great philosophical truths or conceptual designs. Neither symbol nor allegory nor morality belong in this category of art making. Nor was there room for such intellectual elements as composition or theme. Bishop explained her singular and exclusive concern in the following statement:

In this particular kind of artistic expression, the subject must seem unmanipulated—as though a piece of life had been sneaked up on, seized and somehow became art, without anything having been done to it. This is the way it seems, which is part of the content.[10]

She has listed the precedents for this kind of art achievement:

Goya, Rembrandt, Brouwer, van Ostade, sometimes van Gogh, and others, of course, but the list would not be long. Fragonard usually has not this character, I should think. Rembrandt is the only artist of the highest rank to have it. Rubens, who can set the limits on his genius?—nevertheless, he does not have this quality. His drawings are not alive to the utmost—but they express life expanded, and thus, in a sense, manipulated. This is true of Raphael, also, and of Michelangelo.[11]

A successful drawing, she believed, must possess the following characteristics. One, it must be the result of an impulsive, inspired act. Two, it must emerge as if by "magic" or "accident."[12] Three, the desire to seize the instant must become so consuming that the individual elements are inextricably united. Four, the finished work must seem to be a "byproduct of a passionate attack upon the subject matter."[13] Five, it must have a "fortuitous quality."[14]

As a result, despite the fact that she never ventured into the arena of abstract art, Bishop participated in a historic transition in which the dominance of subject matter was undermined, and formal elements were elevated. She explained her point of view:

Now in poetry, a high proportion of the whole meaning is the form itself. After all, you ask, what did the poem say? Well, one would have to recite the poem again. Music—obviously the same is true.

Mozart replied when his patron asked "What does it mean?," 'Oh, it means," and he played it again. . . . Now a painting . . . can have all of the meaning in the form and can function very strongly.[15]

Yet Bishop's belief in the power of abstract form was always tempered by her simultaneous conviction "that abstract art doesn't carry, doesn't deliver quite all the art of painting can deliver."[16] She called art that is all subject "illustration." Subject must coexist with form in order for art to attain its height.

Abstract art . . . can have content without subject. But the content is very generalized. It must be. It can be cheerful, it can be melancholy, it can be energetic or restful or exciting, but it couldn't deliver much of your relation to life, your experience, although aesthetically, it is perfectly sound.[17]

It may appear ironic that some of Bishop's most extraordinary drawings were performed with the rapidity and excitement that one associates with Abstract Expressionism. But these markings are always placed in the service of representation. Bishop seems to have combined the respect for the expressive power of pure form with the tendency among genre artists to submerge the specifics of a subject.

Once again, the derivation of Bishop's approach can be traced to Hildebrand. In discussing the relationship between form and subject, he wrote:

What the artist has to grapple with is a problem of visual manifestations solely. The subjects which he selects for representation need have neither ethical or poetic significance. What he does is to give them an esthetic significance which is distinctive and no less valuable.[18]

In accordance with Hildebrand's theory, Bishop diminished the importance of subject matter and elevated the importance of form. The people who populate her work provide physiognomies, not biographies. Their bodies reflect sunlight, embody emotion, and produce patterns, but they tell no stories. In speaking about her fascination with the bustle of people at the intersection of Fifth Avenue and Fourteenth Street, Bishop reveals an emotional distance from her theme. "This subject enveloped me for years, but I didn't think of them as people, only as layering [of forms]."[19] The people who populated Union Square provided endless combinations of lines and shapes which Bishop spent a lifetime arbitrating. Even the tramps were approached as formal patterns. "They were so beautiful. What marvelous configurations their bodies had . . . and oh, those rumpled clothes."[20]

Union Square, a perpetual arena for figures moving in space, was replete with potential subjects. Typically, Bishop produced preliminary sketches while on the street or while looking out of her studio window. When one of these was chosen as a subject of further development, a systematic procedure was undertaken. The neighborhood shop girls and street bums and other characters who had been observed on the street were invited to come to her studio to serve as models. Here they assumed the same poses that had inspired the original sketches. If they were observed sitting on a curb or leaning on a lunch counter, Bishop would hire a carpenter to construct these props. In this way, the situation on the street was recreated in the studio, providing a controlled environment in which Bishop could attack the same subject time and time again. From morning until evening, day after day, Bishop drew. It was a compulsive, lifelong challenge to "get it right."

Because she reworked the same theme so relentlessly, Bishop devised a method that allowed her to perceive her work with a fresh eye. She would hold a small mirror up to her face and examine the drawing as it was reflected, left reversed with right. This also provided a view of the piece as it would appear as a print. Yet the real source of the continuous intensity of her commitment was her determination to master what she regarded as the central problem—capturing the element of movement.[21] She once stated, "I feel like an explorer. . . . I keep trying it, to find some way, and it keeps me tearing down here to my studio every morning."[22]

Bishop explored every mode of drawing, exploiting the particular qualities of each different medium. Her methods ranged from the sparest delineations to full renderings. The former were pure evocations of shape and contour through line. The latter included references to illumination, surface, and local color. She was as adept at producing descriptive lines, which recorded visual observations, as calligraphic lines, which functioned purely as an expressive force. The power and economy of her ink-laden brush could be set aside in favor of the frenetic scribble of her pen, or the spiral meanderings of the pencil in her later figure drawings. The brusque, karate-like attack of one drawing and the caressing motion of another were all techniques within her repertoire of possibilities. She seemed able to draw upon these divergent approaches to art making, switching visual languages with ease.

In conclusion, it is important to recognize that this remarkable diversity of means was never used in the spirit of a renegade. Bishop may have pursued an independent course, veering away from social realism and also from abstraction. This course produced a range of style but essentially it progressed from the linearity, solidity, and precise draftsmanship of her early work in the 1920s to the loose brushwork, broken contours, and atmospheric quality that enveloped her latest figures, yet her purpose was never to break with tradition. Her vision was not historic. Her role was not pioneering. She seems never to have imagined herself a spokesperson for her generation. Instead, she defined a solitary goal and devoted her life to realizing her own independent purpose. In the process, she produced a compelling body of work that has the look of each decade between 1920 and 1970, but the feel of timeless artistic values.

—Linda Weintraub, Director
Edith C. Blum Art Institute
Bard College
Annandale, New York

NOTES

1. Isabel Bishop, "Isabel Bishop Discusses Genre Drawings," American Artist XVII (Summer 1953): 46–47.
2. Sheldon Reich, *Isabel Bishop* (Tucson, Arizona: University of Arizona Museum of Art, 1974), p. 12.
3. Ibid., p. 20.
4. Ibid., p. 22.
5. Ibid.
6. Ibid., p. 24.
7. Ibid., p. 25.
8. Ibid.
9. Bishop, "Isabel Bishop Discusses Genre Drawings," p. 46–47.
10. Ibid.
11. Ibid., p. 46.
12. Ibid., p. 47
13. Ibid.
14. Ibid.
15. Reich, *Isabel Bishop*, p. 21.
16. Ibid.
17. Ibid., p. 22
18. Ibid., p. 21.
19. *Contemporary American Painting and Sculpture* (Urbana, Illinois: University of Illinois Press, 1963), p. 110
20. Reich, *Isabel Bishop*, p. 13
21. Ibid., p. 23.
22. Ibid., p. 26.

BIBLIOGRAPHY

Bishop, Isabel. "Concerning Edges." *Magazine of Art* 38 (May 1945):168–73.

——. "Drawing the Nude." *Art in America* (December 1963):11.

——. "Kenneth Hayes Miller." *Magazine of Art* (April 1952):162–69.

Bolton, Theodore. *Early American Portrait Draughtsmen in Crayons*. New York: F. I. Sherman, 1923.

Breuning, Margaret. "Bishop Show Emphasizes Solidity." *Art Digest* (May 1949):15.

de Kooning, Elaine. "Isabel Bishop." *Art News* 47 (May 1949):46.

"Drawings of Isabel Bishop." *American Artist* 13 (June 1949):49–55.

Harmes, Ernest. "Light is the Beginning—The Art of Isabel Bishop." *American Artist* 25 (February 1961):28–33, 60–62.

Johnson, Une E. and Miller, Jo. *Isabel Bishop: Prints and Drawings, 1925–64*. New York: The Brooklyn Museum, 1964.

Kimball, Gayle (ed.). *Women's Culture*. Metuchen, New Jersey: Scarecrow Press, 1981.

Lunde, Karl. *Isabel Bishop*. New York: Harry N. Abrams, 1975.

Nemser, Cindy. "Conversations with Isabel Bishop." *Feminist Art Journal* 5 (Spring 1976):14–20.

Paintings by Isabel Bishop; Sculpture by Dorothea Greenbaum. Trenton, New Jersey: New Jersey State Museum, 1970.

Russell, John. "A Novelist's Eye in Isabel Bishop's Art." *New York Times* (April 12, 1975):25.

Sawin, Martica. "Isabel Bishop." *Arts* 30 (November 1955):50.

St. John, Bruce. *Isabel Bishop: The Affectionate Eye*. Los Angeles: Laband Art Gallery, Loyola Marymount University, 1985.

Seckler, Dorothy. "Bishop Paints a Picture." *Art News* 50 (November 1951):38–41, 63–64.

Teller, Susan Pirpiris. *Isabel Bishop: Etchings and Aquatints*. New York: Associated American Artists, 1981.

AN ANTHOLOGY OF DRAWINGS

Study for LOOKING OVER THE WALL, 1928
Pencil and ink, 7½ x 5 inches
Courtesy of Midtown Galleries, New York

LOOKING OVER THE WALL, 1928
Etching, 5⅞ x 4 inches
Collection of Mrs. Walter Fillin

(above)

WOMAN WITH HAT, c. 1925
Pencil, 7 x 5¼ inches
Courtesy of Midtown Galleries, New York

(below)

THE CAP, c. 1925
Pencil, 9 x 6 inches
Private collection

THREE MEN WALKING, c. 1928
Pencil, 8¾ x 6 inches
Private collection

(opposite)

MEN, UNION SQUARE, c. 1928
Pencil, 12½ x 12¾ inches
Courtesy of Midtown Galleries, New York

151

YOUNG MOTHER, 1938
Pen and ink, 4¼ x 3 inches
Private collection

MOTHER AND CHILD, c. 1940
Ink wash, 5 x 5¾ inches
Collection of Dr. and Mrs. John F. Larkin, Jr.

WAITING, 1935
Ink and ink wash, 7⅛ x 6 inches
Whitney Museum of American Art, New York

Study for THE CLUB, 1935
Wash, chalk, pencil, and oil, 16⅜ x 19 inches
Phoenix Art Museum, gift of Mr. Edward Jacobsen, Phoenix, Arizona

WOMAN WITH HAT, c. 1933
Pen, ink, and ink wash, 3⅛ x 4¹⁄₁₆ inches
Collection of Mr. and Mrs. Lowell B. Kramme

YOUNG WOMAN STANDING, c. 1930
Pencil and ink, 7¼ x 4¼ inches
Courtesy of Midtown Galleries, New York

(right)
HEAD OF A YOUNG GIRL, c. 1938
Ink, 3¼ x 2¼ inches
Private collection

THE LETTER, 1933
Ink and ink wash, 9¼ x 6¼ inches
Collection of Elsa and Stanley Sidel

ROSALYND, 1936
Ink and ink wash 4 x 3 inches
Collection of Susan and Herbert Adler

GIRL WEARING HAT, c. 1935
Ink, 3¼ x 2½ inches
Private collection

155

HEAD, c. 1938
Pencil, ink, and oil
15 x 11½ inches
Collection of Michael and
Maryanne Robinson

HEAD #5, c. 1938
Pencil, crayon and chalk
11⅜ x 8¹³⁄₁₆ inches
Wadsworth Atheneum, Hartford,
    Connecticut
Gift of Henry Schnakenberg

A YOUNG GIRL, c. 1940
Ink and pencil, 5 x 2½ inches
Collection of Eric Greenleaf

YOUNG WOMAN, 1947
Ink and ink wash, 5¼ x 4 inches
Private collection

(above middle)
FEMALE FIGURE, c. 1945
Ink and ink wash, 3⅞ x 2½ inches
Collection of Edward DeLuca, Jr.

(right)
SLEEPING WOMAN, c. 1945
Ink and ink wash, 4¼ x 3¾ inches
Courtesy of Midtown Galleries, New York

(opposite left)
THE NEWS, c. 1930
Ink and ink wash, 8⅛ x 2⅞ inches
Private collection

(opposite right above)
THE YAWN, 1937
Ink and ink wash, 5¼ x 5¼ inches
Collection of Mrs. Walter Fillin

(opposite right below)
MAN RESTING ON ELBOW, c. 1937
Ink, 6¼ x 5 inches
Collection of Mrs. Alan D. Gruskin

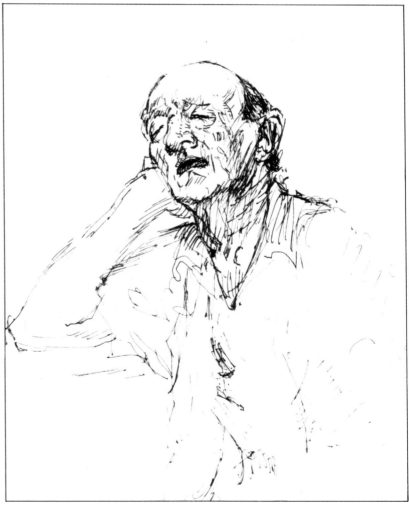

THE SNAPSHOT, 1936
Ink and ink wash, 8 x 6 inches
Private collection

TWO GIRLS AT LUNCH COUNTER, c. 1945
Ink wash, 8¾ x 5½ inches
Private collection

(above left)
READING ON THE SUBWAY, c. 1947
Ink and ink wash, 5¾ x 4¼ inches
Courtesy of Midtown Galleries, New York

(left)
Study for FRIENDS, 1942
Ink and ink wash, 7¼ x 4½ inches
Courtesy of Midtown Galleries, New York

COUPLE ON PARK BENCH #16, c. 1947
Ink wash, 7⅜ x 9 inches
Courtesy of The Frederick and Lucy S. Herman Foundation,
    Muscarelle Museum of Art,
    College of William and Mary, Williamsburg, Virginia

MAN WAITING, c. 1945
Ink wash, 7 x 3¼ inches
Courtesy of Midtown Galleries, New York

SODA FOUNTAIN, c. 1954
Ink wash, 7⅛ x 6 inches
Courtesy of Midtown Galleries, New York

Study for SODA FOUNTAIN WITH
PASSERSBY #2, 1960
Ink wash, 6 x 11¼ inches
Courtesy of Midtown Galleries, New York

(below)

Study for SODA FOUNTAIN WITH
PASSERSBY #1, 1960
Ink wash, 14½ x 23 inches
Courtesy of Midtown Galleries, New York

Study for COKE BREAK, c. 1960
Pen and ink, 7½ x 4½ inches
Collection of The Tennessee Botanical Gardens
    and Fine Arts Center

WOMAN AT LUNCH COUNTER #1, 1965
Ink, 7 x 4¾ inches
Collection of The Tennessee Botanical Gardens
    and Fine Arts Center

Study for COKE BREAK, c. 1960
Pen and ink, 5½ x 4¼ inches
Collection of The Tennesse Botanical Gardens
    and Fine Arts Center

Study for COKE BREAK #1, c. 1960
Pen, 6½ x 3¾ inches
Courtesy of Midtown Galleries, New York

SEATED NUDE, c. 1938
Ink and ink wash, 7 x 6½ inches
Collection of Los Angeles County Museum of Art, Los Angeles, California

STANDING NUDE, 1935
Ink and ink wash, 7¾ x 7½ inches
Collection of Louise R. Noun

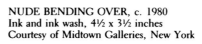
NUDE BENDING OVER, c. 1980
Ink and ink wash, 4½ x 3½ inches
Courtesy of Midtown Galleries, New York

(above)

NUDE DRYING, c. 1960
Pen, 4½ x 3¼ inches
Courtesy of Midtown Galleries, New York

SEATED NUDE, c. 1933
Ink and ink wash, 4¾ x 4½ inches
Private collection

STANDING NUDE #2, c.1980
Ink wash, 7 x 5 inches
Private collection

(right)
NUDE ON BED, c. 1950
Ink, 4½ x 5½ inches
Courtesy of Midtown Galleries, New York

DRYING OFF, c. 1975
Ink, 5¼ x 2½ inches
Courtesy of Midtown Galleries, New York

YOUNG GIRLS, c. 1970
Ink wash, 8½ x 13¼ inches
Courtesy of Midtown Galleries, New York

STUDENTS, c. 1981
Pen and ink wash, 4¾ x 5¼ inches
Courtesy of Midtown Galleries, New York

WOMAN WALKING AND READING, c. 1980
Pen and ink wash, 6½ x 3¾ inches
Courtesy of Midtown Galleries, New York

FOUR PEOPLE WALKING, 1968
Ink, 5 x 5¾ inches
Courtesy of Midtown Galleries, New York

Sketch for SIX WOMEN WALKING, 1963
Oil on canvas, 23½ x 30½ inches
Courtesy of Midtown Galleries, New York

PUBLIC COLLECTIONS

Addison Gallery of American Art, Phillips Academy, Andover, Massachusetts
American Academy of Arts and Letters, New York
Atlanta University, Atlanta, Georgia
Baltimore Museum of Art, Baltimore, Maryland
Brooklyn Museum, Brooklyn, New York
Brooks Memorial Art Gallery, Memphis, Tennessee
Butler Institute of American Art, Youngstown, Ohio
California Palace of the Legion of Honor, San Francisco
Clearwater Gulf Coast Art Center, Clearwater, Florida
Colby College Art Museum, Waterville, Maine
Colorado Springs Fine Arts Center and Taylor Museum, Colorado Springs, Colorado
Columbus Gallery of Fine Arts, Columbus, Ohio
Corcoran Gallery of Art, Washington, D.C.
Dallas Museum of Fine Arts, Dallas, Texas
Davidson College, Davidson, North Carolina
Delaware Art Museum, Wilmington, Delaware
Des Moines Art Center, Des Moines, Iowa
Everson Museum of Art, Syracuse, New York
Fogg Art Museum, Harvard University, Cambridge, Massachusetts
Fort Wayne Art Museum, Fort Wayne, Indiana
Grinnell College, Grinnell, Iowa
Hirshhorn Museum and Sculpture Garden, Smithsonian Institution, Washington, D.C.
John Herron Art Museum, Indianapolis, Indiana
Library of Congress, Washington, D.C.
Los Angeles County Museum of Art, Los Angeles, California
McNay Art Institute, San Antonio, Texas
Metropolitan Museum of Art, New York
Montclair Museum, Montclair, New Jersey
Mount Holyoke College, South Hadley, Massachusetts
Mulvane Art Museum, Topeka, Kansas
Munson-Williams-Proctor Institute, Utica, New York
Museum of Fine Arts, Boston
Museum of Fine Arts, Springfield, Massachusetts
National Academy of Design, Ranger Fund, New York
National Collection of Fine Arts, Smithsonian Institution, Washington, D.C.
Nebraska Art Collection, Lincoln
Nelson Gallery of Art, Atkins Museum of Fine Arts, Kansas City, Missouri
New Britain Museum of American Art, New Britain, Connecticut
Newark Museum, Newark, New Jersey
New York Public Library, New York
Palmer Museum of Arts, Pennsylvania State University, University Park
Parrish Art Museum, Southampton, New York
Pennsylvania Academy of the Fine Arts, Philadelphia
Phillips Collection, Washington, D.C.
St. Lawrence University, Canton, New York
St. Louis Art Museum, St. Louis, Missouri
St. Paul Art Center, St. Paul, Minnesota
Sara Roby Foundation, New York
Springfield Museum of Art, Springfield, Massachusetts
Tel-Aviv Museum, Tel-Aviv, Israel
Tennessee Botanical Gardens and Fine Arts Center, Nashville
Uffizi Gallery, Florence, Italy
University of Arizona Art Gallery, Tucson
University of Atlanta Art Gallery, Atlanta, Georgia
Utah Museum of Fine Arts, University of Utah, Salt Lake City
Virginia Museum of Fine Arts, Richmond
Wadsworth Atheneum, Hartford, Connecticut
Washburn University of Topeka, Kansas
Whitney Museum of American Art, New York
Wichita Art Museum, Wichita, Kansas
Wichita State University Art Museum, Wichita, Kansas
Weatherspoon Art Gallery, Greensboro, North Carolina

GROUP EXHIBITIONS

1936
Whitney Museum of American Art, New York
1938
Virginia Museum of Fine Arts, Richmond
1939
"Golden Gate International Exposition," San Francisco, California
1940
Exhibition of Society of American Artists, New York World's Fair, New York
1942
American Fine Arts Society, New York
Butler Institute of American Art, Youngstown, Ohio
Metropolitan Museum of Art, New York
St. Louis Art Museum, St. Louis, Missouri
1943
Art Institute of Chicago, Chicago, Illinois
1945
Corcoran Gallery of Art, Washington, D.C.
National Collections of Fine Arts, Smithsonian Institution, Washington, D.C.
1946
Library of Congress, Washington, D.C.
1947
Brooklyn Museum, Brooklyn, New York
Carnegie Institute, Pittsburgh, Pennsylvania
1949
Smith College Museum of Art, Northampton, Massachusetts
1950
Whitney Museum of American Art, New York
1951
Pennsylvania Academy of the Fine Arts, Philadelphia
Toledo Museum of Fine Arts, Toledo, Ohio
1955
Corcoran Gallery of Art, Washington, D.C.
Museum of Fine Arts, Boston
1957
Brooklyn Museum, Brooklyn, New York
1959
Fort Wayne Museum of Art, Fort Wayne, Indiana
New York Coliseum, New York
Norfolk Museum of Arts and Sciences, Norfolk, Virginia
1960–61
Virginia Museum of Fine Arts, Richmond
1961
Minnesota Museum of Art, St. Paul, Minnesota
Suffolk Museum and Carriage House, Stony Brook, New York
1962
Hunterdon County Art Center, Clinton, New Jersey
1963
Krannert Art Museum, University of Illinois, Champaign
1965
Gallery of Modern Art, New York
1966
Flint Institute of Arts, Flint, Michigan
High Museum of Art, Atlanta, Georgia
Storm King Art Center, Mountainville, New York
Westmoreland County Museum of Art, Greensburg, Pennsylvania
1967
Krannert Art Museum, University of Illinois, Champaign
1968
Heckscher Museum, Huntingon, New York

1969
Mead Art Museum, Amherst College, Amherst,
    Massachusetts
Oklahoma Museum of Art, Oklahoma City
Tennessee Fine Arts Center, Nashville
Whitney Museum of American Art, New York
1970
Colby College Art Museum, Waterville, Maine
National Arts Club, New York
Joint Exhibition with Dorothea Greenbaum, New Jersey
    State Museum, Trenton
Oklahoma Museum of Art, Oklahoma City
Portland Museum of Art, Portland, Maine
1971
Akron Art Institute, Akron, Ohio
DeCordova and Dana Museum, Lincoln, Massachusetts
National Institute of Arts and Letters, New York
Norfolk Museum of Arts and Sciences, Norfolk,
    Virginia
Weatherspoon Art Gallery, University of North
    Carolina, Greensboro
1972
American Academy of Arts and Letters, New York
Butler Institute of American Art, Youngstown, Ohio
Museum of Art of Ogunquit, Ogunquit, Maine
Wood Art Gallery, Montpelier, Vermont
1973
American Academy of Arts and Letters, New York
Associated American Artists Gallery, New York
Audubon Artists, New York
Minnesota Museum of Art, St. Paul
Philadelphia Art Alliance, Philadelphia, Pennsylvania
1974
Indianapolis Museum of Art, Indianapolis, Indiana
Mount Holyoke College, South Hadley, Massachusetts
Museum of Philadelphia Civic Center, Philadelphia,
    Pennsylvania
National Portrait Gallery, Washington, D.C.
Samuel S. Fleisher Art Memorial, Philadelphia,
    Pennsylvania
1975
Whitney Museum of American Art, New York
1977
American Embassy, London
Brooklyn Museum, Brooklyn, New York
New York University, New York
1979
Middendorf Lane Gallery, Washington, D.C.
Sixth British International Print Biennial, London
Wichita State University, Wichita, Kansas
1981
Associated American Artists, Philadelphia, Pennsylvania
Grand Central Art Galleries, New York
Swain School of Design, Bedford, Massachusetts
1982
Berman Art Gallery, New York
C. W. Post Center, Long Island University,
    Greenvale,New York
Montgomery Museum of Fine Arts, Montgomery,
    Alabama
Richard F. Brush Art Gallery, St. Lawrence University,
    Canton, New York
Rutgers University Art Gallery, New Brunswick, New
    Jersey
Union Square, Open Studios, New York
University of Maryland Art Gallery, College Park
1988
American Academy and Institute of Arts and Letters,
    New York

SOLO EXHIBITIONS

1933
Midtown Galleries, New York
1935
Midtown Galleries, New York
1936
Midtown Galleries, New York
1939
Herbert Institute, Atlanta, Georgia
Midtown Galleries, New York
1942
Midtown Galleries, New York
1945
Smithsonian Institution, Washington, D.C.
1949
Midtown Galleries, New York
1955
Midtown Galleries, New York
1957
Berkshire Museum, Pittsfield, Massachusetts
1960
Midtown Galleries, New York
Virginia Museum of Fine Arts, Richmond, Virginia
1967
Midtown Galleries, New York
1972
Wood Art Gallery, Montpelier, Vermont
1974
Midtown Galleries, New York
University of Arizona Museum of Art, Tucson
Wichita State Art Museum, Wichita, Kansas
1975
Whitney Museum of American Art, New York
1977
Weatherspoon Art Museum, Weatherspoon, North
    Carolina
Mint Museum of Art, Charlotte, North Carolina
1981
Associated American Artists Gallery, New York
Kirkland College, Clinton, New York
Midtown Galleries, New York
1983
St. Gaudens Museum, St. Gaudens, New Hampshire
1984
Midtown Galleries, New York
1985
Loyola Marymount University, Laband Art Gallery, Los
    Angeles, California
1986
Midtown Galleries, New York
1988
Lehman College Art Gallery, Bronx, New York

AWARDS

1936
Isaac N. Maynard Prize, National Academy of Design
1939
Noyes Memorial Prize, Society of American Etchers
1941
Watercolor Prize, Butler Institute of American Art
1942
Adolph and Clara Obrig Prize, National Academy of
    Design

1943
Arts and Letters Award, American Academy of Arts
    and Letters
1945
Third William A. Clarke Prize, Corcoran Gallery of Art
Andrew Carnegie Prize, National Academy of Design
1946
First Pennel Purchase Prize, Library of Congress
1947
Noyes Memorial Prize, Society of American Etchers
American Artists Group Prize, Society of American
    Etchers
1953
Walter Lippincott Prize, National Academy of Design
1955
Benjamin Altman Prize, National Academy of Design
1957
Joseph S. Isadore Medal, National Academy of Design
1967
Benjamin Altman Prize, National Academy of Design
1968
National Arts Club Gold Medal
1970
National Arts Club Gold Medal
1972
Creative Oil Prize, Audubon Artists Annual
1973
Best Oil Award, National Arts Club
1974
Purchase Prize, Mount Holyoke College Art Museum
1975
Creative Arts Award Medal for Painting, Brandeis
    University
1979
Outstanding Achievement in the Arts Award, presented
    by President Jimmy Carter
1982
Skowhegan Governors Award
1987
Gold Medal for Painting, American Academy and
    Institute of Arts and Letters

HONORS

1944
Member, National Institute of Arts and Letters, New
    York
1954
Honorary degree, Doctorate of Fine Arts, Moore
    College of Art, Philadelphia, Pennsylvania
1964
Benjamin Franklin Fellow, Royal Society of Arts,
    London
1971
Member, American Academy of Arts and Letters, New
    York
1979
Honorary degree, Doctorate of Fine Arts, Bates College,
    Lewiston, Maine
1982
Honorary degree, Doctorate, Syracuse University,
    Syracuse, New York
1983
Honorary degree, Doctorate of Fine Arts, Mount
    Holyoke College, South Hadley, Massachusetts

POSITIONS HELD

1936–37
Instructor, Art Students League
1940
Associate Member, National Academy of Design
1941
Academician, National Academy of Design
1946
Vice-President, National Institute of Arts and Letters
(first woman officer)
1956–58
Instructor, Skowhegan School of Painting and Sculpture
1959
Judge, Festival of the Arts, Wisconsin State Park Fair
1961
Represented in Judge the Jury, Virginia Museum of
Fine Arts
1963
Instructor, Skowhegan School of Painting and Sculpture

SELECTED BIBLIOGRAPHY

Books

Austin, Jane. *Pride and Prejudice.* E.P. Dutton & Co.,
1976 (illustrations and afterword by Isabel Bishop).
Bishop, Isabel. *Reginald Marsh: Etchings, Engravings,
Lithographs.* New York: Frederick A. Praeger, 1956.
Contemporary American Painting and Sculpture. Ur-
bana: University of Illinois Press, 1963.
Diamonstein, Barbaralee. *Inside New York's Art World.*
New York: Rizzoli International Publications, Inc.,
1980.
Fine, Elsa Honig. *Women and Art.* Montclair/London:
Allanheld and Schram/Prior, 1978.
Gruskin, Alan D. *Painting in the U.S.A.* New York:
Doubleday, 1946.
Harris, Ann Sutherland and Linda Nochlin. *Women
Artists—1550–1950.* New York: Alfred A. Knopf in
association with the Los Angeles County Museum of
Art, 1976.
Kimball, Gayle (ed.). *Women's Culture.* Metuchen,
N.J.: Scarecrow Press, 1981.
Lunde, Karl. *Isabel Bishop.* New York: Harry N.
Abrams, 1975.
Munro, Eleanor. *Originals: American Women Artists.*
New York: Simon and Schuster, 1979.
Reich, Sheldon. *Isabel Bishop.* Tucson: University of
Arizona Museum of Art, 1974.
Rubenstein, Charlotte Streifer. *American Women Art-
ists.* New York: Avon Books, 1982.
The WPA Guide to New York City. New York: Panthe-
on Books, 1982.

Exhibition Catalogues

"Alan D. Gruskin Memorial Exhibition." New York:
Midtown Galleries, Inc., 1972.
"American Master Prints 1900–1950." New York: Asso-
ciated American Artists, 1986.
"Artist Associated with Art Students League." New
York: Metropolitan Museum of Art, 1951.
"Bishop: Paintings and Drawings." New York: Midtown
Galleries, 1955.
"The Discerning Eye." New York: Associated American
Artists, 1966.
"Isabel Bishop." New York: Midtown Galleries, 1936.
"Isabel Bishop." New York: Midtown Galleries, 1960.
"Isabel Bishop: A Selection of Drawings and Prints."
New York: Midtown Galleries, 1974.
"Isabel Bishop: Drawings and Etchings." New York:
Midtown Galleries, 1935.
"Isabel Bishop: Exhibition of Paintings." New York:
Midtown Galleries, 1933.
"Isabel Bishop: Exhibition of Paintings." New York:
Midtown Galleries, 1967.
"Isabel Bishop: Exhibition of Paintings and Drawings."
New York: Midtown Galleries, 1936.
"Isabel Bishop, Instructor: Life Painting, Composition."
New York: Art Students League, 1936.
Johnson, Una E., and Jo Miller. "Isabel Bishop: Prints
and Drawings 1925–1964." New York: The Brooklyn
Museum, 1964.
Marquesee, Janet. *Painting America: Mural Art in the
New Deal Era.* New York: Midtown Galleries, 1988.
"Midtown Golden Anniversary." New York: Midtown
Galleries, 1982.
"Paintings by Isabel Bishop, Sculpture by Dorothea
Greenbaum." Trenton, N. J.: New Jersey State Mu-
seum, 1970.
St. John, Bruce. "Isabel Bishop: The Affectionate Eye."
Los Angeles, California: Loyola Marymount Univer-
sity, Laband Art Gallery, 1985.
Teller, Susan Pirpiris. "Isabel Bishop." [catalogue rai-
sonné] New York: Associated American Artists, 1981.
———."The Artists of Union Square." New York: As-
sociated American Artists, 1987.
———."Isabel Bishop: Etchings and Aquatints." New
York: Associated American Artists, 1985.
"Twentieth Century American Drawings." Edward Ja-
cobson Collection, 19 .

Periodicals and Newspapers

Alloway, Lawrence. "Isabel Bishop: The Grand Manner and the Working Girl." *Art in America* (September–October 1975).

"American Painters Series: Isabel Bishop." *Scribner's* (November 1937).

"American Painting Bought by the Metropolitan." *New York Herald Tribune* (February 20, 1936).

"Among the Week's Art Shows: Isabel Bishop Exhibits." *New York Sun* (January 21, 1939).

"Art Institute Elects." *New York World-Telegram* (November 19, 1943).

"Art: Two Approaches to the Nude." *New York Times* (April 8, 1967).

Ashton, Dore. [Untitled.] *New York Times* (May 5, 1960).

Bishop, Isabel. "Concerning Edges." *Magazine of Art*, 38 (May 1945):168–73.

———. "Drawing the Nude." *Art in America* (December 1963):11.

———. "Isabel Bishop Discusses Genre Drawings." *American Artist*, 17 (Summer 1953):46–47.

———. "Kenneth Hayes Miller." *Magazine of Art* (April 1952):162–69.

"Bishop at Midtown." *New York Herald-Tribune* (October 22, 1955).

"A Bishop for Herron." *Art Digest* (July 1, 1943).

"The Bishop Girl Seen in Drawing Show." *Art Digest* (June 1942).

"Bishop Pastel Put in Magazine by Error Will Net Buyer $200." *New York World-Telegram* (November 19, 1937).

"Bishop's Progress." *Time* (January 30, 1939).

Breuning, Margaret. "At the Midtown Galleries." *New York Post* (March 16, 1935).

———. "Bishop Show Emphasizes Solidity." *Art Digest* (May 1, 1949):15.

Burrows, Carlyle. "A Dealer's Show of American Art." *New York Times* (July 27, 1941).

"Butler Institute Shows Isabel Bishop's Painting." *Youngstown* (Ohio) *Vindicator* (September 14, 1941).

Campbell, Lawrence. "Isabel Bishop." *Arts* (November 1955).

Canaday, John. "Another Baffler from Audubon." *New York Times* (January 23, 1965).

———. "A Certain Dignity for the Figure." *New York Times* (May 11, 1975).

———. "For Isabel Bishop: It's a Symbol of Endurance." *New York Times* (1967).

Coates, Robert M. "The Art Galleries: Water Colors in Brooklyn." *New Yorker* (May 14, 1949).

"Congress Seceders." *Art Digest* (June 1, 1940).

Cortissor, Royal. "The Spring Show at the Academy." *New York Herald Tribune* (April 12, 1942).

"Craft." *New York Times* (May 8, 1949).

De Knight, Avel. "Isabel Bishop." *France-Amerique* (April 13, 1967).

de Kooning, Elaine. "Isabel Bishop." *Art News*, 47 (May 1949): 46.

Dennison, George. "Isabel Bishop." *Arts* (May 1960).

"The Drawings of Isabel Bishop." *American Artist*, 13 (June 1949): 49–55.

Engle, William. "Portrait of Two Girls Bought by Metropolitan." *New York World-Telegram* (January 21, 1939).

"Exhibition, Midtown Galleries." *Art Digest* (March 1, 1936).

Faulk, Mildred. "Immortalizes Working Girls." *New York Sun* (May 17, 1949).

"First Exhibition of Paintings in Ten Years, Midtown." *Studio* (November 1959).

"First Show Since 1949, Midtown." *Arts* (November 1955).

Forbes, Watson. "Isabel Bishop." *Magazine of Art* (January 1939).

Ford, Donna. "Other Women's Lives." *Worcester* (Massachusetts) *Telegram* (May 20, 1941).

Galligan, Gregory. "Isabel Bishop." *Art News* (April 1987).

Gruen, John. "Isabel Bishop." *World Journal Tribune* (April 7, 1967).

Hakonson, Joy. "Noted Artist Visits Home of Childhood." *Detroit News* (October 13, 1953).

Harmes, Ernest. "Light as the Beginning—The Art of Isabel Bishop." *American Artist*, 25 (February 1961):28–33, 60–62.

Harrison, Helena A. "A Long Career but Still a Fresh Eye." *New York Times* (October 12, 1980).

Hess, Thomas B. "Big Business Taste: The Johnson Collection." *Art News* (October 1962).

———. "The Miracle of Union Square." *New York Magazine* (May 19, 1975).

"Isabel Bishop." *Pictures on Exhibit* (December 1940).

"Isabel Bishop." *Time* (November 28, 1955).

"Isabel Bishop Finds Critics Receptive." *Art Digest* (February 1, 1936).

"Isabel Bishop Finds Time for Both Art and Family." *Peekskill* (New York) *Star* (May 1, 1941).

Istomin, Eugene. "Isabel Bishop." *Current Biography* (October 1977).

"Italian King Buys U.S. Art." *New York Times* (April 9, 1942).

Jewell, Edward Alden. "Art in Review." *New York Times* (May 19, 1942).

Jordan, Philip Harding. "An American Master." *Eatontown* (New Jersey) *Sentinel* (May 13, 1943).

Kerr, Adelaide. "Isabel Bishop Paints Four Pictures in Year." *Toledo* (Ohio) *Times* (May 2, 1943).

Lane, James W. "Bishop." *Art News* (June/July 1942).

Lenson, Michael. "Romanticists at Trenton." *Newark Sunday News* (May 17, 1970).

McBride, Henry. "Attractions in the Galleries . . . Midtown Galleries." *New York Sun* (May 6, 1942).

———. "Isabel Bishop." *New York Times* (May 22, 1942).

Mattison, D. M. "Tidying Up by Bishop." *John Herron Institute Bulletin* (June 15, 1943).

"A Miller Pupil's Shackles Loosen." *Art Digest* (March 1, 1936).

"Miss Bishop Rates High as a Painter." *New York World-Telegram* (February 15, 1936).

Moore, Sally. "Isabel Bishop: Half a Century of Painting the Flotsam of Union Square." *People* (May 26, 1975).

"National Academy Picks Winning Art." *New York Times* (1952).

Nelson, Dona and John Mendelsohn. "An Interview with Isabel Bishop." *Issue: A Journal for Artists* (Fall 1985).

Nemser, Cindy. "Conversations with Isabel Bishop." *Feminist Art Journal*, 5 (Spring 1976):14–20.

New Lexington (Ohio) *Daily Record* [Column] (October 28, 1937).

"New Paintings Shown by Isabel Bishop." *New York World-Telegram* (January 21, 1939).

New York Sun [Column] (May 22, 1942).

New York World-Telegram [Column] (February 5, 1944).

"Notes and Comments on Events in Art." *New York Herald Tribune* (January 22, 1939).

"Other Women's Lives." *Philadelphia Bulletin* (September 8, 1943).

"Paintings and Drawings Shown at Midtown." *Art Digest* (May 1, 1949).

"Perlez, Jane. "Daily Closeup." *New York Post* (April 1, 1975).

"Poet in the Square." *Time* (May 16, 1960).

Pomeroy, Ralph. "Isabel Bishop." *Art News* (April 1967).

Preston, Stewart. "Sculpture by Nakian: Recent Painting by Dufy, Bishop and Peck." *New York Times* (May 8, 1949).

Russell, John. "A Novelist's Eye in Isabel Bishop's Art." *New York Times* (April 12, 1975):25.

Sawin, Margica. "Isabel Bishop." *Arts*, 30 (November 1955):50.

Sayre, A. H. "Substantial Technique in Bishop's Work." *Art News* (February 22, 1936).

Schuyler, James. "Isabel Bishop." *Art News* (May 1960).

"Seated Nude by Isabel Bishop at Metropolitan." *New York Herald Tribune* (November 6, 1942).

Seckler, Dorothy. "Bishop Paints a Picture." *Art News* (November 1937):50.

"Some Others Who Arouse Interest: Displays by Gropper, Sepeshy & Bishop." *New York Sun* (February 15, 1936).

"They Drink and Fly Away." *Time* (May 23, 1949).

"Two Approaches to the Nude." *New York Times* (April 8, 1967).

Weisburg, Ruth. "Webs of Movement and Feeling." *Artweek* (March 1985).

Wilson, William. "The 9–5 Girls of Old New York." *Los Angeles Times* (March 21, 1985).